Only Love

Living the Spiritual Life in a Changing World

by
Sri Daya Mata

A publication of
SELF-REALIZATION FELLOWSHIP
Founded in 1920 by Paramahansa Yogananda

ABOUT THIS BOOK: This volume began as a small booklet published in 1971 entitled *Qualities of a Devotee*. It contained several talks by Self-Realization Fellowship president Sri Daya Mata, most of which were given in the 1960s. The present expanded anthology spans a twenty-year period, from 1955 to 1975, with selections ranging from major addresses in India and America to brief informal talks. Also included are some of Daya Mata's candid responses to questions asked of her during *satsangas* (gatherings of truth-seekers at which the leader speaks extemporaneously on spiritual subjects). Many of the talks first appeared in print in the pages of *Self-Realization* (the magazine begun by Paramahansa Yogananda in 1925). Although most of them were directed either to members of the Self-Realization Fellowship monastic order or to students of Paramahansa Yogananda's teachings, people of all different faiths and walks of life found them to be a source of helpful and compassionate guidance. Thus, in 1976, Self-Realization Fellowship published this first anthology of Sri Daya Mata's talks; a second volume, *Finding the Joy Within You*, was published in 1990.

Authorized by the International Publications Council of
SELF-REALIZATION FELLOWSHIP
3880 San Rafael Avenue • Los Angeles, CA 90065-3298

Self-Realization Fellowship was founded by Paramahansa Yogananda as the instrument for the worldwide dissemination of his teachings. The Self-Realization Fellowship name and emblem (shown above) appear on all SRF books, recordings, and other publications, assuring the reader that a work originates with the society established by Paramahansa Yogananda and faithfully conveys his teachings.

~ *First Edition 1976, First Paperback Printing 1995* ~

Library of Congress Catalog Card Number: 75-44633
ISBN 0-87612-215-2 (hardcover)
ISBN 0-87612-216-0 (paperback)

Printed in the United States of America on recycled paper ♻
11590-54321

To my revered Gurudeva
PARAMAHANSA YOGANANDA
without whose blessings
this devotee would not have found
God's love divine—the perfect, all-fulfilling
love of Him who is our one Father, Mother,
Friend, Beloved

ABOUT PARAMAHANSA YOGANANDA

"The ideal of love for God and service to humanity found full expression in the life of Paramahansa Yogananda....Though the major part of his life was spent outside India, still he takes his place among our great saints. His work continues to grow and shine ever more brightly, drawing people everywhere on the path of the pilgrimage of the Spirit."

—from a tribute by the Government of India upon issuing a commemorative stamp in Paramahansa Yogananda's honor

Paramahansa Yogananda is widely revered as one of the preeminent spiritual figures of our time. Born in northern India in 1893, he lived and taught in the United States for more than thirty years—from 1920, when he was invited to serve as India's delegate to an international congress of religious leaders in Boston, until his passing in 1952. Through his life and teachings, he contributed in far-reaching ways to a greater awareness and appreciation in the West of the spiritual wisdom of the East.

Paramahansa Yogananda's life story, *Autobiography of a Yogi,* is at once a fascinating portrait of this beloved world teacher and a profound introduction to India's ancient science and philosophy of Yoga and its time-honored tradition of meditation. A perennial best-seller since it was first published nearly fifty years ago, the book has been translated into eighteen languages and is used as a text and reference work in many colleges and universities. Considered a modern spiritual classic, it has found its way into the hearts of millions of readers around the world.

Today Paramahansa Yogananda's spiritual and humanitarian work is being carried on by Self-Realization Fellowship—the international religious society he founded in 1920—under the guidance of Sri Daya Mata. In addition to publishing his writings, lectures, and informal talks (including a comprehensive series of lessons for home study), the society oversees temples, retreats, and centers around the world; the monastic communities of the Self-Realization Order; and a Worldwide Prayer Circle.

PREFACE

By Chakravarthi V. Narasimhan
Under-Secretary General for Inter-Agency Affairs
and Coordination at the United Nations

I came across *Autobiography of a Yogi* in 1967. It was my first introduction to Paramahansa Yogananda and to the Self-Realization Fellowship movement. I have since followed closely the work of this society. I have had the privilege of meeting several times with Sri Daya Mataji, and with some of her dedicated colleagues. I have also had the opportunity to visit the Self-Realization Center in Encinitas, California, where Paramahansa Yogananda lived for many years.

As I said earlier, it was my privilege to meet Sri Daya Mataji; for anyone who has been in her presence cannot fail to be affected by the aura of spiritual peace and serenity that she radiates. Sri Daya Mataji was moved at a very young age to follow the teachings of Paramahansa Yogananda; obviously, the divine spark of illumination emanating from her Guru had touched her even in youth. She became one of the first followers of Sri Yoganandaji during his lifetime, and is now his worthy spiritual successor in carrying his message not only in this country and my own, but across the world.

This message of peace and inner tranquillity, and of an integrated human personality, is most relevant to our times. We live in an age of turmoil, and the pace of change is indeed frightening. Even in the most advanced nations many human beings feel insecurity at the individual level, while in the countries of the third world there is unimaginable poverty, want, and suffering. We need a new philosophy of interdependence and global solidarity to resolve these problems. This requires a very considerable change of attitude, not merely on the part of governments operating through an international organization such as the United Nations, which I have served for over nineteen years, but even more importantly at the level of the ordinary individual. We need, more than ever before, human beings who are integrated individuals, and Self-realization is a sure and simple way of achieving this integrated personality.

When the first moon astronauts saw the earth from the moon, they exclaimed that it was so beautiful. From that distance they saw the earth, not as countries or continents or regions inhabited by people of different races and colors, but as a whole. If we are not able to see the earth as a whole, it is because we are so earthbound in our thinking. This is a limitation we can easily overcome by the exercise of a little imagination, which will enable us to lift our sights over the narrow divisions that tend to separate us, and to follow the teachings of the great saints and sages who have urged us to practice love and compassion and tolerance.

The message of Sri Daya Mataji is therefore one of great importance and relevance in this age of doubt and skepticism. Her talks published in this book stand out as a beacon of hope and faith. They are a proclamation, not only of the oneness of the human race, but also of the oneness of man with God.

New York City
14 January 1976

INTRODUCTION

To read or hear the words of Sri Daya Mata is to become acquainted with one who is in love. Overcoming exclusiveness at every level, hers is a love that reaches out and embraces all. It is a sublime expression of the soul's yearning and of its joyous fulfillment in God. In this volume of informal talks, Mataji gives us a glimpse into the realm of expanded spiritual consciousness wherein the soul experiences the love divine.

Daya Mata was born in Salt Lake City, Utah. From her earliest years she felt deeply drawn to God. At the age of eight, when she first heard about India in school, she felt a mysterious inner awakening, and with it a conviction that India held the key to the fulfillment of her life. That day, when school was over, she ran home and exclaimed jubilantly to her mother, "When I grow up I will never marry; I will go to India." Prophetic words from a child.

When Daya Mata was fifteen, she was given a copy of the Bhagavad Gita, "Song of the Lord." This scripture deeply moved her, for it revealed God's compassionate love for and understanding of His children. He was seen to be approachable, knowable; and His children were called divine beings, who through self-effort could realize their spiritual birthright, oneness with Him. Daya Mata resolved that somehow, in some way, she would devote her life to seeking God. She went from one religious authority to another, yet always there remained in her heart an unsatisfied question: "But who *loves* God; who *knows* Him?" Sadly she realized that she lacked the one essential to her search: the guidance of someone who actually knew God.

It was in 1931, when she was seventeen, that Daya Mata first saw Paramahansa Yogananda.* He was addressing a large audience in Salt Lake City. Recalling her first impressions, she has said, "How can I describe it to you? When I saw him standing there on the platform, I became absolutely transfixed. He was speaking of the spiritual potential of will power, and of love for God. He spoke as I had never heard anyone speak of God. I was enthralled. Instantly recognizing him as one who knew God and who could show me the way to Him, I resolved, 'Him I shall follow.' "

In a crowd of thousands it seemed unlikely that Daya Mata would have any opportunity to meet the Guru. But it is said that adversity is sometimes a blessing in disguise. Daya Mata had long suffered from a severe blood disorder. The illness, which doctors had been unable to cure, had finally forced her to leave school. However, she was faithfully attending Paramahansaji's classes, and the bandages covering her swollen face had apparently attracted the attention of the great Guru. Toward the end of the classes he told the

* Paramahansa Yogananda, author of *Autobiography of a Yogi*, had been in the United States since 1920. At that time he had been invited as a delegate from India to the International Congress of Religious Liberals in Boston. During the intervening years, he had lectured throughout the country, and had established in Los Angeles an international headquarters for his work, Self-Realization Fellowship/Yogoda Satsanga Society of India.

audience that within seven days no trace of her illness would remain. And so it was. But to Daya Mata, an even greater blessing than her remarkable healing was an opportunity to meet this man of God. She was extremely shy, and to this day wonders how she found the courage to speak her first words to him: "I want so much to enter your ashram and devote my life to seeking God." The Guru looked at her penetratingly for a moment. "And you will."

But it would require a miracle for that to come to pass, as family opposition was great. She was still a young girl, and her family—with the exception of her understanding mother—was firmly set against her leaving home to follow a religion wholly foreign to them. But one evening, Paramahansa Yogananda said in his lecture that if a devotee called deeply enough to God, with determination to receive a response, His response would be forthcoming. Daya Mata made her resolve; and that night after the family had retired, she went into the living room, where she could be alone. Tears flowed as she poured out her heart to God. After several hours, a profound peace came over her whole being, and she could cry no longer: she knew that God had heard her prayer. Within two weeks all doors were opened, and she was able to join the ashram of Paramahansa Yogananda in Los Angeles.

Time sped by quickly at the feet of her Guru. Although she was deeply happy, those early years of ashram training were not without struggle. Paramahansaji was lovingly but firmly engaged in the task of transforming the young *chela** into an exemplary disciple. He later told Daya Mata that he gave to her in those

* Hindi word for "disciple."

years the same severe discipline that his guru, Swami Sri Yukteswar, had given to him—a significant remark, since she was to inherit the spiritual and organizational mantle Sri Yukteswar had bestowed on him.

With the passage of time, more and more responsibility was given to Daya Mata by the Guru. Several years before his *mahasamadhi*,* Paramahansaji asked her to take administrative charge of the Mount Washington international headquarters. He then retired into seclusion and began to devote most of his time to writing. Daya Mata's spiritual and administrative responsibilities became increasingly greater as the worldwide activities of the society grew.

The time came when the Guru told his disciple that he would soon leave his earthly body. Stunned, Daya Mata asked how the work could continue without him. Softly he answered, "Remember this: When I have left this world, only love can take my place. Be so drunk with the love of God night and day that you won't know anything but God; and give that love to all." These words became the guiding light of her life.

Paramahansaji entered *mahasamadhi* in Los Angeles on March 7, 1952. Three years later, succeeding the late, saintly Rajarsi Janakananda, Sri Daya Mata became the third president of her Gurudeva's society. As the spiritual successor of Paramahansa Yogananda, and a true "Mother of Compassion," as her name signifies, she sees to the faithful carrying out of his ideals and wishes concerning Self-Realization Fellowship/Yogoda Satsanga Society of India, the spiritual guidance of its

* A God-realized soul's conscious exit from the body at the time of physical death.

members, and the training of the monastic disciples who reside in the various Self-Realization/Yogoda Satsanga ashrams.

Though her life is given primarily to her Guru's work and to devotees of the path of Self-Realization, she feels all seekers of God to be a part of her spiritual family, whatever their creed. A Catholic Sister of Charity, after meeting Daya Mata and hearing her speak on several occasions, remarked, "For me, as a member of a religious order, Daya Mata is a shining example of what a life committed to the service of God and neighbor ought to be. She makes me think of that great forerunner of Christ, John the Baptist, who said of himself, 'I am the voice of one crying in the wilderness. Make straight the way of the Lord.' In her presence there are no Catholics, Protestants, or Hindus, but only children of the one Father, God. And each one of them she receives graciously and has a place for them in her heart. I, a Catholic nun, have experienced so much her kindness and her interest and encouragement. I always felt that she treated me as one of her own. For me she will always be an ideal of what my life as a religious ought to be. . . . She radiates God."

Not the rule, but the spirit of the path to God is the effective, almost magical ingredient that transforms the life of the devotee. Scriptural truths and injunctions are merely words until they become a part of one's thoughts and actions. They must be lived. *Only Love* illustrates the spirit of divine seeking. It lays the foundation for a life of attunement with God, who is the Source, Sustainer, and Essence of man's life and being.

All spiritual seekers, whatever their outer role in life, will find that this book speaks to the soul. Though many of the talks in this collection were addressed primarily to the resident monastics of Self-Realization/Yogoda Satsanga ashrams, the truths expressed herein are universally applicable.

Daya Mata's words, illumined by direct personal realization, show that seeking God is a joyous experience; finding Him is Joy Itself.

SELF-REALIZATION FELLOWSHIP

Los Angeles, California
March 1976

CONTENTS

ILLUSTRATIONS

FOLLOWING PAGE

ONLY LOVE

Why Should We Seek God?

Jyoti Mandram Hall, Bangalore, India, December 31, 1967

Why should we seek God? What is God? How can we find Him?

The first question can be answered very simply. We should seek God because we are made in His image,* and only His perfection and permanency can give us lasting happiness.

Man was given a mind and a body with five senses through which he perceives this finite world and identifies himself with it. But man is neither the body nor the mind; his nature is spirit, the immortal soul. As often as he tries to find permanent happiness through his sensory perceptions, so often his hopes, his enthusiasm, his desires, are shipwrecked on the rocks of deep frustration and disappointment. Everything in the material universe is essentially ephemeral and ever changing. That which is subject to change carries within it the seeds of disappointment. And so it is that our ship of worldly expectations sooner or later runs aground on the shoals of disillusionment. Therefore we should seek God, because He is the fountainhead of all wisdom, all love, all bliss, all contentment. God is the source of our being, the source of all life. And we are

* Genesis 1:27: "So God created man in His own image...."

made in His image. When we will find Him, we will realize this truth.

If God is the goal of man, then what *is* He? Every scripture, and every great soul who has ever spoken of his experience of God, has declared certain qualities to be the nature of Spirit. Still we cannot say what God is. No man has ever been able to describe Him fully. There is a story that an image made of salt went down to the shore to measure the depths of the ocean. The moment it stepped into the water, it melted away. The image could not measure the depths, for it had become one with the sea. It is the same with man. His very being consists of those same qualities that are of Spirit. The moment his soul becomes identified with the Infinite Being, he becomes one with God, and can no longer describe what God is. But many saints have described what one experiences when he communes with Spirit.

All scriptures state that God is peace, love, wisdom, bliss. All agree that God is cosmic intelligence, omniscient and omnipresent. He is the Absolute. He is the great cosmic sound of *Aum,** the Amen of the Christians. He is cosmic light. These are all attributes or qualities of the Infinite. And when the devotee deeply seeks Him, he begins to perceive these various manifestations of the Divine.

* *Aum:* The basis of all sounds; universal symbol-word for God. *Aum* of the Vedas became the sacred word *Hum* of the Tibetans; *Amin* of the Moslems; and *Amen* of the Egyptians, Greeks, Romans, Jews, and Christians. *Aum* is the all-pervading sound emanating from the Holy Ghost (Invisible Cosmic Vibration; God in His aspect of Creator); the "Word" of the Bible; the voice of creation, testifying to the Divine Presence in every atom. *Aum* may be heard through the practice of Self-Realization Fellowship methods of meditation.

It is said that the first proof of God's presence within man is peace—that peace which cannot be affected by anything external. When man pins his dreams, his ideals, his hopes, and his ambitions on worldly goals, the peace that he feels from their accomplishment is only temporary. This world is a world of duality: life is made up of pleasure and pain, health and sickness, heat and cold, love and hate, life and death. Man's goal is to take his consciousness beyond this law of duality, this veil of *maya*,* and find the One who is present in all creation and beyond creation.

"How Can We Find God?"

The next question is: "How can we find God?" He cannot be known through the senses, nor measured by the limited twelve-inch ruler of the intellect. As often as we try to discover His bliss, love, wisdom, and joy in sensory experiences, so often are we disappointed. But when man learns by deep meditation to still his body and shut off the five senses, a sixth sense, intuition, begins to express itself. God can be known only through the sense of intuition. He *wants* us to know Him. Hence every man is endowed with intuition.

The first aim, then, is to quiet both body and mind, that the whispers of intuition may be heard. Our guru, Paramahansa Yogananda, taught us those techniques of concentration and meditation by which the body and mind can be stilled, thereby enabling us to commune directly with the Infinite. Yet how many have

* "Cosmic illusion; literally, 'the measurer.' *Maya* is the magical power in creation by which limitations and divisions are apparently present in the Immeasurable and Inseparable."—Paramahansa Yogananda in *Autobiography of a Yogi*.

said to me in my travels around the world: "You are fortunate; you can do this, but I have bad luck. God does not respond to me." If God does not respond it is because the devotee does not feel sufficient yearning for Him and has not learned how to meditate deeply. Master* told us: "When you sit for meditation you must strive to empty the mind of all physical and mental burdens and restlessness. You must forget the body, and you must forget self-will. These are vital steps that religionists of all spiritual paths must practice in order to commune with God. How can this be done? By the practice of yoga techniques of concentration."

We were trained by Guruji to have one little corner in our rooms reserved only for meditation, for the thought of God. And we were taught to throw everything else out of our minds the moment we sat quietly in that "temple." We have to do it at the time of death, do we not? In an instant all of the engagements that we think are so important in this world, the care of the body which preoccupies us so much of the time, must be forsaken when death calls us. Therefore no duty in this world is more important than our duty to God, because no duty here can be performed without the power that comes from God. So when you sit to meditate, empty the mind of all troublesome thoughts. It can be done if you learn how to concentrate.

The next point is that the devotee must develop humility. Unless and until we learn to forget our-

* The nearest English equivalent to "Guru." "Master," "Guruji," and "Gurudeva" are titles by which a disciple signifies his loving respect when addressing or speaking of his guru, or spiritual teacher. "Master" in this sense describes one who has mastered himself, and is therefore qualified to lead others to self-mastery.

selves, we can never fill the consciousness with the thought of God. The I, I, I-consciousness must go. We must learn and practice that humility which is spoken of in the Bhagavad Gita:*

> Uprightness, heed to injure naught which lives,
> Truthfulness, slowness unto wrath, a mind
> That lightly letteth go what others prize;
> And equanimity, and charity
> Which spieth no man's faults; and tenderness
> Towards all that suffer; a contented heart,
> Fluttered by no desires; a bearing mild,
> Modest, and grave, with manhood nobly mixed,
> With patience, fortitude, and purity;
> An unrevengeful spirit, never given
> To rate itself too high—such be the signs,
> O Indian Prince! of him whose feet are set
> On that fair path which leads to heavenly birth!

Humility is surrender of one's self, of heart, mind, and soul. It is surrender of the complete man at the feet of the Divine. How to practice this? Be like the devotee who follows the path of *Karma Yoga;*† offer the fruits of all your actions at the feet of God. Hold always this thought: "Lord, Thou art the Doer; I am nothing. Thou art the Light that shines in the bulb; I am only the bulb."

The next step is to practice patience. When we sit for meditation we must rise above all consciousness of time. Even if we meditate only for five minutes, those five minutes must be one hundred percent concentrated upon God. The mind should not think of any-

* Chapter XVI:2–3, Sir Edwin Arnold's translation, *The Song Celestial.*
† Union with God through right action.

thing external, but go deeper and deeper within until the waters of peace, bliss, and love divine slowly begin to well up within our consciousness.

We must also be content with small steps. Don't expect great experiences in the beginning when you meditate. Be content with the slightest glimpse of the Divine within—a sense of quiet peace deep in your consciousness.

One of the reasons some persons cannot meditate deeply is that they are anxiously seeking a happy experience, and become discouraged if they do not feel an immediate response from the Divine. The Lord tests us in this way. He doesn't come to His devotees unless and until He is convinced beyond any doubt that their love for Him, their yearning for Him, is unconditional. When He knows that we mean business with Him, that we cannot be placated by any lesser gift He may send to us, then He gives Himself. Guruji often said: "We must be like the naughty child. When the baby cries, the mother gives it playthings, hoping to satisfy it so that she can go about her household duties. But as often as the mother gives the naughty child toys, he picks them up and throws them on the floor and goes on crying for the mother. To that child the mother must respond." It is the same with the Divine: so long as the Cosmic Mother sees that we are satisfied with a gift, She will go on dropping playthings to us and keep Herself away. But if we are able to convince Her of our sincerity by the constancy of our devotion, by our unconditional love, by our humility and self-surrender, crying, "Mother, no longer can we be satisfied with Your toys; we want only You!" then the Divine Mother responds to us.

When you meditate in a hurry or with anxiety, the

very object of your meditation, the Divine One from whom you are seeking a response, escapes the net of your concentration. The secret of seeking God in meditation is to abandon restlessness, impatience, and anxiety.

The Rewards of Meditation

What are the fruits of a deep meditation? First of all, man becomes a peaceful being. No matter how life treats him, his consciousness remains centered within the Self. Krishna taught Arjuna to become anchored in That which is changeless. The only changeless principle in creation is God. Everything else is subject to change because it is only a dream-thought of His. You and I seem so real, these bodies so substantial; the whole world appears to be quite permanent. Yet this seeming reality is nothing but condensed thoughts of the Cosmic Dreamer. Like Him, the moment we take our minds away from this world, it exists no longer for us. The moment we put our minds on the Infinite, we begin to perceive the natural state of our souls as individualized expressions of the Cosmic Self.

If God is love, peace, wisdom, joy, then we, being made in His image, have the same nature. But who knows himself as such? Every night when we go to sleep, for a few brief hours the Infinite Beloved in His compassion permits us to forget this body with all of its worries and troubles. But when we awaken in the morning we immediately put on again the consciousness of a finite being, bound by many limitations, habits, moods, and desires. So long as we are thus tied, we cannot know ourselves as the soul.

The only way that we will ever be able to break the

fetters, the hidden cords that bind us to this fleshly form, is by meditation. And the first proof of the existence of God within ourselves is that we gradually begin to feel a great sense of inner tranquillity.

As we go on meditating deeper and deeper, the consciousness begins to expand. There awakens a longing to forget this little fleshly form and behold the Self in all beings. We want to do for others; the desire arises to selflessly serve mankind.

As one meditates regularly throughout his life, he begins to perceive the great ocean of love that lies within himself. Devotion for God brings us to that state wherein we know Him as Cosmic Love, expressing Itself through all human manifestations of love. Without the love that comes from Him we could not love anyone. Without the power that comes from Him we could not even think or breathe. Yet we shut out of our life the very One upon whom we are dependent every minute of our existence and cling to this world as our own.

God Is the Common Denominator of All Life

You may say, "Is it essential, then, that I forsake the world and go away to some hidden cave to seek God?" Not at all. Wherever He has placed us in this world, there we must draw Him: by selflessness, by meditation, by striving all the time to practice His presence in our life. In short, we should reduce life and all its activities to a common denominator. God is that common denominator. Instead of shutting Him out of all our activities we should include Him in everything we do—eating, sleeping, working, loving all our dear ones—by always thinking of Him as the Cosmic Beloved of our souls.

God is the simplest to love, when we learn to seek Him in the depths of true devotion. Without devotion plus meditation He cannot be known; but He is the easiest in the world to know when like a child we silently call upon Him in the depths of our consciousness. For a little while every day, every human being should devote some time to deep meditation, forgetting the world, seeking Him, talking to Him in the language of the heart. Our Guru often said to us: "Everything in this universe belongs to my Beloved. But even that all-possessing Beloved One is seeking something, crying for something. That 'something' is your love. Unless and until you go back to Him you will suffer; and at the same time He also suffers, because He craves your love."

So the goal of mankind is to find God, and, finding Him, to realize freedom from all worldly cares and sufferings. In freedom is the experience of tremendous love, of blissful union with the Cosmic Beloved. This is the goal of life. And the way to this goal is selfless deep meditation.

When you sit to meditate, forget everything. In India many who have sought God have gone to cremation grounds to meditate long and deeply, because there they are reminded of the bare reality of worldly life; it has no meaning, for every man regardless of his achievements in this material world must one day lay his body down as a lump of clay. So when you sit to meditate, think to yourself: "I am dead to the world. I am dead to my family. I am dead to all my duties. I am dead to these senses. I am dead to everything finite. Only my Beloved exists for me." With that consciousness, meditate deeply and call upon Him.

Because man is God's highest creation, it is an insult to yourself and to Him when you give all your attention to things of the world. So long as you feel that you cannot find time for God, you may rest assured He will have no time for you. He is always waiting for your invitation, but as our Guru used to say, "God is very shy. He will not come unless He knows that you want Him." That is why you feel in your life a great void; a great sense of uselessness and futility. You will go on feeling that lack, you will go on suffering until you awaken from your dream of delusion and realize that without Him you cannot exist. When you begin to understand that He alone can satisfy your heart, you will also gradually begin to feel His sweet response; not before.

In the Gita* Lord Krishna declares that just a little practice of meditation will save man from dire suffering in this world. So meditation should be as vital a part of the day as eating. Man doesn't hesitate to look after the body; he sees that it is fed, he clothes it, and he gives it regular rest. But how he neglects the Self! He is not the body; yet much of his time, effort, money, and interest are spent in looking after the little fleshly house in which he lives for just a few years. What an insult to the soul!

No wonder man suffers in this world. He deserves to suffer, and he will go on suffering until he shakes himself out of this delusive dream. Man was not put here merely to be born, to grow up, reproduce, and die. Animals do this. Man was blessed with superior intelligence, the power of discrimination, and the power of

* II:40.

free will. No other creature of God has these qualities. To ignore them or misuse them is foolish. We are not animals; we are divine beings, images of God, and we will suffer until we manifest those spiritual qualities with which He has endowed us.

Lord Krishna told his beloved disciple Arjuna: "Get away from My ocean of suffering."* Man is still striving to prove to himself that this world is not an ocean of suffering, but he will never be able to do so. Sometimes we feel sure we have caught the butterfly of happiness, but in the next instant it has darted away from our hand. Why not concentrate on the soul bird-of-paradise that resides in the bodily cage? Nourish it a little bit every day with the only food by which it can live: devoted meditation. We should say: "I will selfishly keep aside at least one hour a day to nourish you, my soul. I will forget the world for that one hour."

Paramahansaji's guru, Swami Sri Yukteswar, was very fond of this chant, in which God is speaking to His devotee, asleep in the dream of worldly delusion:

> "O My saint, wake, yet wake!
> You did not meditate, you did not concentrate,
> And passed thy time in idle words.
> O My saint, wake, yet wake!
> Death will be at thy door,
> And you won't have time anymore
> To redeem thy soul.
> O My saint, wake, yet wake!"†

* "Him will I swiftly lift forth from life's ocean of distress and death, whose soul clings fast to Me. Cling thou to Me!" (Bhagavad Gita XII:8, Sir Edwin Arnold's translation).

† From *Cosmic Chants,* a book of devotional songs to God, by Paramahansa Yogananda.

Therefore pray unceasingly: "O soul, wake thou from thy dream. Wake, sleep no more! Wake, sleep no more!"

It is said that there is only one difference between a saint and a sinner: the saint went through the same trials but refused to give up. Constantly take the name of the Divine inwardly, not in an absentminded way, but as Guruji taught us: "The moment you utter His Name within, let your whole thought and devotion flow that way." Ever be whispering to the Cosmic Beloved: "Will that day come, when just uttering Thy Name, my whole being will be aflame with love?"

When that time comes, the devotee finds a different meaning in life. It becomes a joyous experience. Everywhere he looks he sees a reflection of his Beloved; and in the midst of adversity he learns, as Gurudeva said, to "stand unshaken midst the crash of breaking worlds." He realizes, "I am the soul; fire cannot burn me, swords cannot pierce me, water cannot drown me. I am That."

To live life in this way is to find freedom wherein you cannot be bound by anything. In the midst of all life's experiences you will find that you are in the loving, protecting arms of the Beloved of your soul.

Man's Expanding Horizons

Self-Realization Fellowship Ashram Center, Encinitas, California, May 18, 1963

Man is ever striving to expand the scope of life. He is exploring the unknown, and reaching farther and farther into the Infinite, in a material way, through his flights around the earth and into outer space, and by plumbing the depths of the oceans. He is developing his mind through applied science and the invention of such remarkable machines as the computer. Every day new vistas are opened, and he is forced to expand his mental horizon to keep pace with his own achievements. How much more is required of man's brain today than in the time of our grandfathers!

Man's spiritual nature is also undergoing a transformation through expansion. He is probing more deeply into that Mystery which some call God, or Brahman, or Allah, or yet other reverential names—the one divine, cosmic, intelligent, all-loving, all-joyful Being who is our Creator and Sustainer. Religious experience, not mere belief, is the demand of today's seekers.

This trend further convinces me of the very special part the work of Paramahansa Yogananda's Self-Realization Fellowship has to play, not only in the West, but all over the globe. I see this confirmed by tremendous worldwide interest in Paramahansaji's

Autobiography of a Yogi and in the *Self-Realization Fellowship Lessons.**

Followers of Self-Realization have an important role in this work and in the world. Their supreme responsibility is to become living examples of truth, for their own salvation, and for the enlightenment of others. Do not be discouraged if at times you feel you are standing still rather than progressing on the path. Make greater effort! You have but one duty, which was constantly stressed by Paramahansaji when he was with us: improve yourself by finding your Self. Though our temples be filled with millions, unless there is qualitative spiritual growth within those followers, such an organization will not touch the heart of our Guru. He had no interest in large followings unless they were crowds of really God-seeking souls. His greatest interest, his only interest, in each human being who came to him, was to help that devotee to realize consciously the divine link between his soul and God. The link is already there; the role of a true guru is to help the devotee to become consciously aware of his oneness with God, the creator of his soul and of this universe.

When I think of these sublime principles, I become intoxicated with enthusiasm for Guru's work, and even more so with enthusiasm to be drunk with the divine consciousness of God night and day. He is the only reality, the one thing that is unchanging and everlasting in this world.

* The teachings of Paramahansa Yogananda, sent to students throughout the world; available to all earnest truth seekers. These lessons contain the yoga meditation techniques taught by Paramahansa Yogananda. In addition, they explain universal laws that govern all life, and how man may operate them for his highest welfare.

Daya Mata with Paramahansa Yogananda,
SRF Hermitage, Encinitas, California, 1939

"Since I first set eyes on my guru, Paramahansa Yogananda, almost forty years ago, it has been my joy to lay my heart, my mind, my soul, my mortal form, at the feet of God, in the hope that somehow He might use this life I have given to Him. Such soul satisfaction has filled these years; it is as though I am constantly drinking from the fountain of Love Divine. I can take no credit for this; it is the Guru's blessing, a blessing he bestows on all of us in the same way, if we but prepare ourselves to receive it."

Satsanga (spiritual gathering) at SRF international headquarters, in Los Angeles, on eve of departure for tour of SRF European centers, August 1969

"Like almost everyone else in this active world, I have never had the opportunity to be wholly free from activity. But I made up my mind at the beginning that every free moment was going to be filled with God."

If you please the whole world, so that everyone is at your feet, what then? If you have all the riches the world can offer, what then? Everything we pursue externally leads eventually to satiation, and after satiety comes boredom. The only experience that gives complete fulfillment, complete contentment, that can never satiate or bore us, is communion with the ever-new, ever-joyous Lord.

The peoples of the world are feeling the need for God and will turn to Him. The more tormented the world is, the more we realize we cannot do without Him! I remember the period that began in 1939, when the world was echoing increasingly with sounds of hatred and war. My inner torment at that time was great. I can think of nothing more senselessly painful than war—I used to suffer as if all its wounds were within myself. Anyone who is sensitive, who has sympathy or compassion for others, feels this way. Whenever we would drive with Guruji between our Encinitas ashram and Mount Washington,* and see those young boys in military service lined by the side of the road asking for rides, all I could think was, "Each of you is someone's child." One day Paramahansaji looked around and saw the pain in my face. He read my mind. The car was not full, so he said: "Stop a minute." There were two boys, just young lads, by the side of the road, and he said: "Do you want to ride with us?" I can never forget how sweet Guru was to them. A simple act, but it eased my anguish.

During this period of war Paramahansaji said: "It seems as if the world is going backward, as if it will

* Site of, and, by extension, a frequently used name for the international headquarters of Self-Realization Fellowship in Los Angeles.

destroy itself by hate. But know this for certain: the world is on the upward trend, constantly evolving, constantly improving."

White stands out against a black background. In the same way, goodness shows up most prominently against a background of evil; the light of God shines brighter against a background of great darkness. Was this not also true during the time of Christ? The Bhagavad Gita* declares that when the world is filled with the darkness of ignorance, the Divine sends one of His saints to earth to restore righteousness by showing man the way to uplift his consciousness.

The Experience of God Will Bring World Unity

Self-Realization Fellowship teaches respect and love for all religions, all races, all peoples; for God is One and there ought to be unity among His children in the consciousness of Him. It is not so much what we believe about God that will give us individual Self-realization and ultimately world unity, but rather what we experience of God. Whether we are clothed in a black, brown, yellow, red, or white body is of absolutely no interest to God. He wants only to see how we, whom He made in His image, will respond to Him in His variously colored forms. Can't you see there is no difference? that the skin color, the race, the religion does not alter the divine soul-image of God within each man?

We have to struggle to break down prejudices, which narrow the mind and consciousness and cause the Divine in us to weep. Even so, we can blame part of

* IV:7–8.

our shortsightedness on God. We can say to Him, "Lord, it is You who have dropped this thought of division into the minds of men, for they could not have thought it unless You first conceived it. Man is no more than a part of Your dream of creation." Everything is of God; in the highest sense, even the evil force is His tool. Evil, or *maya,* is the cosmic delusion whose shadows, like a motion picture film, transform the creative light of God into countless individualized forms. Without *maya* there would be no creation. In this metaphysical sense, evil is any form of darkness that hides or distorts the ever perfect light of God's presence everywhere in creation.

What is the reason for creation? As Paramahansaji taught, it is the Lord's *lila* or divine play. Do not give it so much importance. Do not become so absorbed in His *lila* that you forget Him who created the play, who is its very Substance.

Man's Proximity to the World Blinds Him

If you close one eye and hold a penny very close to the other eye, you cannot see the world beyond: you become blinded by that little object. If you move the penny away from your open eye, you see how vast the world is. So it is with God. When you are too closely identified with the world, you become blinded by it, and cannot see Him. Overwhelmed by anxiety, worry, fear, insecurity, and uncertainty, you cannot begin to imagine that God exists.

It is only when you push the "penny" of this world away from you that you see the vastness of God within and beyond creation. Only then do you behold the world in its true perspective. You have to keep that which is most important—God—directly in your line of vision. When He is first, everything else will fall into proper focus.

For that reason Christ said: "But rather seek ye the kingdom of God; and all these things shall be added unto you."* This message Paramahansaji stressed again and again to all. Each human being feels in his heart the need for something. We need God; we need to hold on to something changeless that will give us strength to cope with the particular problems, trials, and experiences we attract to ourselves. Never blame anyone else for what happens to you. Blame yourself; but don't punish yourself, for that is wrong. And never indulge in self-pity; that also is wrong. Always remember this: You are the child of God, and meditation is the way by which you can realize you are His.

Meditation is the constant affirmation of what we are. When we sit to meditate, we are affirming: "I am the soul, one with God." When you practice the Self-Realization methods of meditation, you are striving to remember your real nature. Like anything else, the more you practice meditation and the more proficient you become, the more you will gain from it; the more you will remember and express your divine heritage. The importance and value of meditation lie in its inviolable promise of this ultimate realization of your soul nature.

It is not enough to go to church; it is not enough to hear the wonderful sermons given in Self-Realization Fellowship temples. Sermons are good; it is important to hear them. If you are able, you should attend services

* Luke 12:31.

regularly. But in addition there must be daily practice of the presence of God, daily communion with Him in deep meditation, daily taking of your problems to Him.

Don't Wait Until Life Forces You to Seek God

I don't know how the world lives without such communion with God. It may well happen that the world will be so beaten down that it will be forced to think of God. But even that will be good, because ultimately it makes no difference how we are brought to our knees before the Lord, so long as we are before Him.

Therefore never bemoan what happens to you. Never feel defeated by any circumstance of your life. Strive always to think, "Lord, I have faith that no trial or experience comes to me without Your permission. I know I have within me, through Your blessing, the strength to cope with anything that comes." Even when your task seems superhuman, remember that the Divine is just stretching the rubber band of your consciousness, expanding its potentially infinite capacity.

With this attitude of faith and surrender, one learns to pass through this world with one sustaining thought, "You, Lord—You, You, You." The devotee feels so much a part of God that he relates every experience to God. Whether he is involved in world affairs, busy in his office, or showing love for husband, wife, or children, he realizes it is all God—from God and for God.

When one has that sacred attitude wherein he strives to see God in his relationship with husband, wife, children, brothers, and sisters, and knows that in each relationship it is possible to behold another facet of God's nature, he begins to find that he lives, moves, and has his being in the one Divine Beloved.

Such is the purpose of life, the goal of every human being. By clinging to the consciousness of God as we pass through all the experiences life brings, we once again behold ourselves, and everyone around us, as part of the Infinite Whole. Then freedom is ours.

Our Divine Destiny

India, date and city unknown

Man has a divine destiny to fulfill, but few are those who know the goal of their existence, and fewer still are those who earnestly seek the attainment of that goal. The average life is spent in caring for the needs of the body, in fulfilling responsibilities imposed by the necessities of the moment. In this way the average man lives and dies, knowing not whence he came, why he is here, and whither he will go.

The great world scriptures aver that man is the most inspired creation of the Divine, that he is in fact made in the image of his Creator. Is the image of God a body of flesh prone to disease and powerless against death, an intelligence shrouded in *maya* and subject to changing moods and emotions? This cannot be the image of the Great Power that conceived and sustains the cosmic intricacies of the Universe! Where, then, is the divine image in which man is supposed to be made?

Man is a threefold being. He has a body, but he is not that body which demands and suffers and dies. He has a mind, but he is not that mind which is perverted by the tricks of cosmic delusion. His real nature is the immortal *atman,* the soul, which dwells invisible in the temple of mortal flesh. This *atman* is the image of God within man—the all-perfect image whose godly qualities are love, wisdom, omnipotence, and joy eternal.

Blind is the child of God who permits the desecration of that divine image within him, so obscuring it with the imperfections of matter consciousness that it can no longer be recognized. By so doing man lives against his real nature. This is why he is never fully satisfied, why there is always some longing deep inside that drives him down first one path and then another, seeking that ever-elusive, unknown quantity.

The "something else" that man is seeking is God: the Divine One who throbs just behind the beat of the heart; the Love that percolates through all forms of love for family, friends, and beloved; the Joy that ignites all flames of happiness; the Wisdom omniscient that sits just behind the thoughts of the little human mind. Nearer than the nearest is the Divine Power that has given man life, and can bring meaning and fulfillment to his existence.

Man's Destiny Is to Know God

Man's divine destiny, then, is to find God and to realize that His image lives within the temple of the mortal body and mind. Finding Him within through realization of the Self or *atman,* we find the Cosmic Beloved in all manifestations of nature and in His formless Self as *Sat-Chit-Ananda:* ever-existing, ever-conscious, ever-new Bliss. When the God image within awakens to the glorious realization that it is a reflection of the omnipotent, omniscient, omnipresent Lord, what then shall man crave? What love will his heart yearn for, what attainment will be beyond his grasp, what joy will elude him? Man must realize that he himself is the reflected Source of all fulfillment, love, and joy.

*Raja Yoga** is the ancient science that teaches the way to know the Self and to reunite that individualized image of God with the Cosmic Spirit. In meditation we regain our forgotten heritage as the children of the Cosmic Creator. All things that the Father has, we as His children may also have as we reestablish our true relationship with Him. Behind all pursuits and desires, happiness is the treasure we seek. He who follows faithfully the path of meditation begins to realize this truth: "From Joy I have come, in Joy I live, move, and have my being, and into that sacred Joy I shall one day melt again."

He who would know this Joy must strive to fulfill the divine destiny of his life here on earth. He must devote himself to rediscovering his true nature and the relationship of that Self with Spirit. He need not fly away from his responsibilities in the world; but out of the twenty-four hours of each day he can surely give one hour to seeking God. According to the depth and steadiness of one's effort, even a few minutes' daily devotional practice of the yoga meditation techniques taught by our great Gurus† will enable the sincere devotee to attain the ultimate blessings. As we draw nearer to God, and as we increasingly manifest our real nature, life itself changes in aspect. Even trials are seen as but the shadow of God's hand, outstretched in blessing. A greater strength of purpose and power of direc-

* The "royal" or highest path to God-union, *Raja Yoga* includes the essentials of all other forms of yoga. It stresses scientific meditation techniques as the ultimate means for attaining God-realization.

† The line of God-realized Gurus of Self-Realization Fellowship/Yogoda Satsanga Society of India: Mahavatar Babaji, Lahiri Mahasaya, Swami Sri Yukteswar, and Paramahansa Yogananda.

tion motivate our actions. Above all, peace and joy become the center of our existence—a core of inner bliss around which revolve all our thoughts and experiences.

We must one day return to the Source of our being. Why prolong our exile in delusion? Krishna said to his beloved devotee Arjuna: "Get away from My ocean of suffering and misery." Let us "get away" by following the path of the Great Ones. Let us strive from today toward the destined goal of our existence. Let us seek Self-realization, let us seek God, let us attain!

Qualities of a Devotee

Self-Realization Fellowship international headquarters, Los Angeles, California, February 19, 1965

The first requirement on the spiritual path is a sincere yearning for God. Without that yearning, it is impossible to know Him. In any pursuit there must be a constant drive in order to succeed. If you would know the Divine, there must be a similarly persistent longing for Him.

But even yearning is not enough in itself; we must go further. Once the yearning for God arises, it must be nourished by loyalty and dedication; first, to God, and then to the path and to the teacher whom God sends you. When the devotee begins to seek God earnestly, he finds a path and a guru who inspires him along that path. So the second important point is loyalty and dedication to God, and to the guru whose path one chooses.

Now the third requirement is vital: As we proceed along the spiritual path, we should strive to behave in such a way that we inspire others who may be weak, rather than contribute to their negation or discouragement. This does not mean that we should be eager to draw others' attention to ourselves. But we should conscientiously manifest in our lives the spiritual qualities we begin to feel in our hearts; by so doing we shall be able to encourage others along the path to God.

The fourth point is that the devotee must strive constantly for humility, because humility is like a valley wherein the waters of God's grace can gather. Egotism, the consciousness of I, I, I all the time, is like an arid desert mountaintop; no water can gather on such a peak. It collects in the deep valleys. Similarly, the waters of mercy, of grace and blessing, gather only in the valley of humility, wherein the devotee puts God first and himself last. Then, as in the Hindu saying: "When this 'I' shall die, then will I know who am I."

The fifth requirement for a devotee is to set aside a time every day for meditation. You are fooling yourself—and you may think that you are fooling God, but you are not—if you pretend in any way that your work is more urgent than your daily efforts in meditation. This misconception is one of the great tests faced by the devotee. In the beginning, we may not feel any tangible results in meditation, and so we are inclined to consider first the demands of our work or of this world. It is only when we face bitter experiences, reverses, and physical, mental, or spiritual suffering that we suddenly begin to see that we have made a mistake in our failure to put God first in our lives.

Keeping the Mind on God Helps Solve Your Problems

Whenever we came to Paramahansaji with any kind of personal problem or complaint—if we had criticisms to make, or found ourselves in conflict with other persons or our work—he did not dwell on that particular matter. In fact, with one exception, I cannot remember his sitting down and talking with me about my problems. We disciples never came to him for private consultations, because we knew what his answer would be. "Just keep your mind here," he used to say, pointing to the Christ center between the eyebrows, the seat of spiritual consciousness and of the divine eye.* "Keep your attention here, and keep God in your consciousness." Perhaps to some persons it would seem that he did not give us what we were looking for; after all, it might be expected that a guru would give his disciples long discourses about spirituality, the nature of God, the value of virtue. But usually he would say just those few, quiet, effective words. And for those who were receptive, this was all that was needed. In this way he taught us that when we straighten out our own consciousness, we invariably find the right solution to our problems.

Master was a sublimely simple person, as are all great lovers of God. He had only one request, and one lesson he wanted us to learn: that God should come first in our lives. We should keep before our consciousness the words of Christ: "But seek ye first the kingdom of God, and His righteousness; and all these things shall be added unto you."† He did not intend this counsel only for those who live in monasteries, but for all mankind. If we dwell on this truth—*seek God first*—we gradually begin to understand what it means. When we have a pain in the stomach, when we are experiencing trouble with our family, or when we are having difficulty in our work, the solution is very simple: Pinpoint the mind on God. Become anchored in Him first, and then from that level of consciousness try to solve your problems. You will be amazed how quickly and effec-

* The spiritual eye; the center of spiritual perception and intuitive wisdom in man.

† Matthew 6:33.

tively it works. I know, because this is the way I have lived and carried out my many responsibilities all these years.

Work at Changing Yourself

Sometimes devotees become so enthusiastic about their own spiritual conversion that they want to tell everybody else about it and change them too! They are so sure that they are doing good, and that they themselves have changed for the better, that they want to convert the whole world. Such enthusiasm is chiefly external. The main effort should be to convert oneself. It is a difficult thing to change the self, because it is so deeply embedded in a crust of habits we are not even aware of. We are held prisoner, bound by our own particular thoughts, moods, and emotions.

It is not easy to change the habits you have formed during a lifetime of perhaps thirty or forty years. Try to change even one little habit and see how difficult it is! Tell yourself not to talk too much; tell yourself not to gossip; tell yourself not to be critical; tell yourself not to be jealous. After some effort you may feel: "It seems impossible for me to change. Is there no hope for me?" Certainly there is hope. But that hope will never be fulfilled so long as you strive only to change the people and situations around you, instead of working on your own flaws. That is what I beg you to learn. Long after the lips of all of us here are sealed, the eternal truth in these counsels will still be applicable.

You *can* change yourself, and the way is by seeking God sincerely, by meditation, and by self-discipline. There is no other method. It takes the combined power of all these to overcome bad habits and to destroy those deep, hidden subconscious fetters that have made us prisoners in these limited physical bodies and minds.

This is the reason some rules are necessary for devotees on the spiritual path. There is need for rugged discipline. Do you think it is easy to know Him who is the Master of this universe? Do you think it is simple to commune with Him when the mind is filled with meanness, negation, gossip, hatred, lack of faith—with anything less than God? Never! Without meditation and self-discipline to remove these obstacles, you cannot know Him.

God can be known only if there is total surrender to Him. Do not be satisfied with being a mediocre disciple. Do not set your standards by the rest of the world. I remember Guruji's saying to a group of us: "I do not want mediocre devotees on this path. That is why I am hard on you all. I want to see who has the fiber to go all the way to God."

His last personal words to me—how I treasure them! —were uttered three days before his *mahasamadhi.* We were coming down together in the elevator here at the headquarters. "Poor child," he said, "I have been very hard on you in this life.* I gave you the same hard discipline that my Guru gave me. I saw that you could take it. But remember, he scolded me because he loved me." And then he said something so poignant, "But I won't be here much longer to give you this discipline."

I replied, "Master, throughout eternity, any time

* Reference to the previous incarnations when guru and *chela* had been together. Paramahansaji knew that Daya Mata had an eminent role to play in this incarnation, and he was spiritualizing and strengthening her for that responsibility. An explanation of the law of reincarnation is given in a footnote on page 50. *(Publisher's Note)*

you feel this devotee needs your discipline, do give it to me. I know you can guide me even when your form is no longer here. Please always continue to do so!"

I have no wish to cater to this physical or mental self. I am seeking freedom, and that is what I want for every one of you.

When Attitude Is Right It Becomes Christlike

"When this 'I' shall die, then will I know who am I." When the attitude of the devotee is right, it becomes Christlike. No one could insult Jesus, no one could destroy his loving spirit or rouse his ire, because his consciousness was anchored not in the little self but in the Greater Self, God. And so he was never offended by anything or anyone.

Suppose the whole world accuses us unjustly. When the mind is secure in God, what the world thinks is of little importance. This does not mean you should scorn the world, but that you should be so immersed in the One Consciousness (and perhaps you all have had a glimpse of it) that you feel compassion for people and try to understand them. Above all, you know only one thing: "If the whole world praises me, but I do not feel the blessing of my God, I am bereft of any comfort. But if the whole world reviles me, yet I feel the strength of my God behind me, I am sublimely fulfilled in Him."

That realization is what the spiritual life is all about. And as long as I live, I shall keep trying to pull my consciousness, and the consciousness of every one of you, back to that One Goal. I want to see Gurudeva Paramahansa Yogananda's message bring solace to all; the hives of organizational work should be filled with the honey of God-loving souls.

Every human being wants to be free. Once you become aware that you are really a prisoner in this life, you will crave freedom. I was born with that longing, and I would not let anything stand in the way of my search for freedom. If I did not get it, I knew I could not blame anyone else. Now, nothing can interfere with my relationship with God. People might try to deter me, or think they can influence me to leave this path, but they will never be able to do so. Why? Because I know what I want. I try never to deceive myself, and I do not delude myself with yearnings for anything of this world. God comes first.

When the devotee has that consciousness, his life becomes so much easier. It becomes anchored and stable. He knows and feels his true relationship with other people, and everything in his life focuses into the right perspective.

To seek God first does not imply that one has to renounce the world. Blessed are they who can do it. But wherever the devotee is, he can put the Lord first, and then all the rest of his duties and relationships will fall into their proper place. After all, there is only one source of love, not half a dozen. There is only one Dynamo, not three or four, whence wisdom, love, and joy come. Their one source is God.

When the devotee becomes more deeply united with the Lord, he realizes that he is merely an instrument, a part, of that great Source. He sees everything and every other human being as part of that common Source. As a result, his relationships with other people become correct. He no longer feels a need to demand anything from them. He no longer wishes to clutch, to grab, or to whine for love, kindness, and understanding. Rather, he wants to give. He knows the divine law that what one gives in this world, he will get back. It is a science; it never fails.

When you sow kindness, you will reap kindness. But if you have been kind to someone for years, and he has given you nothing but hurts, remember that in previous existences you have sown seeds of unkindness that are now bringing forth their just fruits. You have to be patient; wait for the seeds you sow now to bear fruit in their own season. You cannot plant a seed today and get a fruit tree tomorrow. In its own time the seed will produce a tree. Plant good habits today, scatter kindness in this world today; in their own time they will produce worthwhile results. If the fruit you are reaping today is sour, do not lament about it, or feel self-pity. You yourself have sown the seeds that are producing that sour fruit. Accept the situation like a man, so to speak. Stand up and take unpleasantness with courage and patience. Take it with faith in God.

Everyone Is a Little Bit Crazy

The trouble is that all of us, as Paramahansaji used to say, are a little bit crazy, and we do not know it; because people of like peculiarities mix together. No human being is really balanced until he knows God. The only "well-adjusted" persons in this world are those who have attained Self-realization—and that is what we are all striving for.

Many people are a little bit off mentally, but many, many more are off emotionally—emotionally crippled, emotionally immature. You cannot deny it. It seems to me that this emotional sickness is the main problem of mankind today. One symptom of it is evident in the way people constantly blame outer conditions or other people for their various troubles. "Well, if he had not done this, or if she had not said that, I would not be suffering today." Nonsense! The fallacy of such reasoning is one lesson that Master very definitely insisted we learn.

Do not blame others for the way you are. Your situation is exactly what you yourself have created. The statement, "You are the master of your own fate," is absolutely true. You are the designer of your own destiny. The difficulty is that in our ignorance we have not known how to control our human weaknesses, and have therefore put into motion those modes of behavior that have brought upon us the ill effects we experience today. Realization of this truth is a sign of mature thinking. It favors our emotional growth. I am stressing this because the right attitude toward our problems is a basic need for everyone.

We all have to grow up, and growing up means to recognize and behave as our true Self: "I am not this emotional individual. I am not this fearful and whining person. I am not this insecure weakling. I am a part of God." Guruji tells us that by practice of regular meditation, and by following the spiritual rules he set forth, we will realize who we truly are. When we become fully aware of God, when our consciousness becomes one with His, only then will we know.

Grasp Truth with the Intellect; Absorb It Within the Soul

If you want to change yourself, you have first to understand certain important points intellectually, and then begin to absorb them deeply in your soul. Suppose you want to develop devotion. Write that word on a piece of paper, or copy down some thought that arouses your devotion, and post it on your door or in some other conspicuous place where you will see it often. Every time you look at this reminder, try not only to grasp intellectually the concept of devotion, but to feel what it means. Ponder it, let it influence you with instant ardor. Master used to say: "You have to churn the ether with your love for God, with your yearning for Him." Converse with God, feeling that you are churning the ether with your prayer.

For instance, we have just sung one of Guruji's chants, "Door of My Heart." When I finish chanting aloud, that is not the end for me. One should progress from loud chanting to whisper chanting, and then to mental chanting. When I finish a chant, my attention does not suddenly stop there. I go deeper and deeper and deeper in the thought I have been chanting: "Wilt Thou come, O Lord, wilt Thou come; just for once come to me?" My heart cries. My mind becomes withdrawn and, as Guruji advised, I "churn the ether" with that thought. In other words, a chant must be repeated again and again with ever-increasing feeling, so that the meaning of the words you are repeating becomes a part of your consciousness. You can do this only if your attention is one hundred percent on what you are doing. If your attention is ninety-nine percent on God, but you are thinking a little bit about the people around you, or are harboring a stray thought about your work, you won't be able to achieve success in attracting the divine response.

Guruji used to say to us, "God will not come to you unless you give Him one hundred percent of your attention." If you think that you can progress just by sitting and practicing *Kriya** while the mind is darting here and there, you are mistaken. There are some who reason, "Today I have done a hundred *Kriyas;* I should be advancing fast. . . . This week I have done a thousand *Kriyas;* I should be almost fully developed spiritually." Nonsense! Such a devotee does not have the right attitude. He is like Guruji's aunt; for forty years she had been saying her prayers on her beads daily, but her mind was always elsewhere. No wonder she at last complained that she was getting no response! You must mean business in order to get God in this life. You *can* succeed in that aspiration; but not without the proper degree of effort.

God Is Shyly Evasive

The Lord is very hard to know. He runs not only this universe, but millions of other universes. How can you think He will have time for you unless you go after Him in earnest? Master used to say that you must learn to "milk" the silence in deep meditation to draw the hidden Consciousness, the secret, loving Intelligence residing everywhere within this creation.

That is not easy. God is shyly evasive, always hiding; and you are always being sidetracked. Too frequently your mind is occupied with aimless thoughts: "This is more important; that is not important," or "I

* A special yogic technique of meditation practiced by Self-Realization Fellowship members. *Kriya Yoga* is a sacred spiritual science, originating millenniums ago in India. It includes certain techniques of meditation whose devoted practice leads to realization of God. Revived in this age by Mahavatar Babaji (see page 184), *Kriya Yoga* is the *diksha* (spiritual initiation) bestowed by the Gurus of Self-Realization Fellowship.

like this face; I dislike that face. This person is so kind to me; that one is so mean. Look what this person is doing, and just see what that one did." Where is the one-pointed mind? How will you find the Lord in all this mental debris? When you close your eyes and take that last breath in this life you will be the same as you are now, having made no progress whatsoever. Then you will say: "Beloved God, I have wasted my time. I did not want to do that. I was so close to the doors of infinite fulfillment, but I have frittered away my golden opportunity."

The tragic thing is that we put other considerations before God because we are afraid we are going to miss something in this world. This is the great delusion. We fear that if we give ourselves to God, we might lose something else. "Well, now, let me see," the mind reasons, "I might miss out on all that life offers. There are so many things I would like to have; I want love, I want power, I want to be known, I want to do great things in this world." These are what we think we want. We cannot deny it; all mankind is pursuing these goals. But how foolishly! We go after them in the wrong way.

Our Basic Desires Are Native to the Soul

Why do we want fame? Why do we want power? Why do we want love? Why do we want joy? We crave these things because they are a part of our true nature, the nature of the soul. The full realization of this was part of an experience I had in India when I was meditating at Babaji's cave.* The soul is immortal. And what is fame but the fulfillment of an innate desire to go on

* See page 184.

living in the memory of the rest of the world. Why shouldn't the soul want to leave behind on earth the name and achievements of one of its incarnations for others to read about a thousand years from now? The soul is all-powerful, one with the omnipotence of God. Why shouldn't it want to express its potential? The soul is love and joy. So it is natural to seek these also as essentials of life.

You see from this that we pursue goals native to our being. The delusion lies in expecting fulfillment from a world that is nothing but a fleeting dream. The world is a fraud; I see this so clearly. Why be tossed about on the waves of remembrance and forgetfulness, of life and death? Why waste yourself that way? And for what reason? All the things that man is seeking, he will find in God. The trouble is, we do not have enough faith in the divine promise that if we seek God first, all other things will be added unto us. But I have believed this all my life; I know it to be so. *I know it.* Any time doubt arises, hold to that thought. Ask God to prove it to you. And you will see, if you do your part, that He will prove it to you. That proof is a marvelous thing!

Whenever any kind of delusion comes into your life, any kind of temptation or trial, just remember these words: "I seek You first, my God, and I know that all other things will be added unto me." Believe that. You have to start with believing, and then eventually, if you go on seeking Him, you will suddenly say: "My goodness! All that I wanted, I feel I have; I have not missed anything."

Most people do not want to seek God because they are afraid they might have to give up this or that. What are you giving up? You really relinquish nothing. You find all fulfillment within your soul. You feel divine love in your heart. You realize all wisdom within you. You feel celestial strength. You no longer look for anything, for you have no unfulfilled desires.

Have not all the great ones who have ever communed with God—from Krishna, Buddha, Jesus, to our Masters*—proven in their lives the all-fulfillment of God; sufficiently so that they would rather die than let go of Him? Most people, by contrast, would rather die than let go of the world; how desperately they cling to this world and all the things in it. But once you have found God, you would rather die than renounce Him. There is the difference. Because those who know Him are convinced that "all other things" have been added unto them. They know and they feel God's all-inclusiveness. The world can never give the satisfaction that God will give. And no human love will ever bestow the infinite joy that is found in God's love.

There will always be disappointments, disillusionments, and heartaches in life; because the nature of the soul is perfection, while everything on earth is gross and limited. Here, you find the inability to convey adequately to others what you feel; the inability of others to receive what you want to give; the inability to explain through words (words are too crude!) what the soul wishes to tell.

Everything we are seeking is in God. Hold to that one thought for a while—for the next six months, for example. Say to yourself: "Just think! seek God first, and all other things will be added unto me." Meditate on it. Every time you feel tempted or discouraged or dis-

* The line of Gurus of Self-Realization Fellowship.

tracted, say to Him, "God, I am giving my life to You. Now, I am holding You to Your promise." And you will see that He does keep His word. The point is that you should have a working relationship with God; do not be satisfied until you do. You can develop that relationship by following these rules that I have given to you from Master's teachings.

There will always be an inexplicable yearning and void in man until he gets back to God. You may travel the whole world over, you may seek throughout the entire universe, you may gather all the experiences creation has to offer, but you will remain "lost" until you get back to Him.

No amount of trying to fill one's heart with human love will ever satisfy; there will always be a lack of some kind. And it is logical that it should be so. Christ said: "My kingdom is not of this world."* Your kingdom, too, is not of this world. Therefore, so long as you fool yourself into thinking you can build your hopes and happiness in this world, they will be dashed on the rocks of disappointment. This is truth I am telling you. You know it in your soul.

To create a working relationship between you and the Infinite, there has to be an effort on your part, an unstrained effort, through which the mind dives deeper and deeper within. The time comes when you will churn the ether with just one thought: "You, You, my God, my Love, only You, only You, only You." The mind becomes totally immersed in that consciousness. The soul begins to open up; you feel a flood of joy and devotion, and a great wave of understanding that

* John 18:36.

only the Lord is real. You know, at that moment in the presence of God, that you are facing Truth. Only God is Reality.

What I have said to you tonight can be summed up in these words from the Bhagavad Gita:* "He who perceives Me everywhere, and beholds everything in Me, never loses sight of Me, nor do I ever lose sight of him."

* VI:30.

Understanding One Another

Self-Realization Fellowship international headquarters, Los Angeles, California, December 14, 1965

We should behave always according to our true nature as divine children of God. No matter what others do to hurt us, we ought to return forgiveness and compassion. We have the power to change others' feelings toward us if we practice that. With heartfelt sincerity the hand of love and friendship should be offered to all. If the hand is slapped, or as often as it is slapped, it should be proffered again. If that person continues to reject you, withdraw for a time, but silently continue to send him your loving thoughts. Be ever ready to extend the hand of friendship again, when an opportunity arises.

Receive praise or blame without becoming excited about either. Though at times it may be difficult to cope with persons who are critical of us, we should not ignore what they say, if it is constructive. Sometimes it is all right to try to explain ourselves, to make every effort to come to an understanding. But often it is a waste of time to go into long explanations, which may sound only like justifications. In such instances we are wiser merely to accept silently.

The best attitude is that divine humility referred to by St. Francis of Assisi when he said, "Accept blame, criticism, and accusation silently and without retaliation, even though untrue and unjustified." Even if what is said about us is untrue, even if we feel it is unjustified, we are spiritually ennobled when we accept it without argument and without retaliation. Leave the judgment to God. One who would know God must strive first to please Him, not man.

The time to explain, the time to remain silent, depends upon the circumstances. But there is never a time to retaliate, under any circumstances. Always let God be the judge. His laws are just, so in the highest sense we need never defend ourselves.

There will be those who praise and understand us; there will be those who blame and misunderstand. We should take both evaluations in stride. Our part is to strive always to the best of our ability to live by truth. When we realize we have made a mistake, we should instantly ask the Divine to forgive us; and then correct ourselves.

It is no use trying to hide our errors from God; He knows them anyway. We can trustingly tell Him all our mistakes and seek His help in righting them. God's immanence makes Him a constant, divine companion with whom we can freely share our feelings. He sees us as we are. How can we feel egotistical about ourselves when we know we are nothing without Him? Once we realize this, there begins within us a persistent struggle to reach perfection in His eyes. The person who is satisfied with himself ceases to grow spiritually. Egoistic self-satisfaction is a grave sin against the higher Self. Whosoever ceases to strive for improvement shrinks in spiritual stature.

Any time we are wrong, let's admit it. Let us not always think we have to be right. This is not being honest with ourselves. The fact that we believe a certain way does not necessarily make it right. If someone shows us we are wrong, we should be willing and ready to change. This is the way we grow and acquire understanding. Long explanations of why we erred are unnecessary. We need simply say, "I am very sorry. I didn't understand it that way."

Without Communication, Misunderstanding Grows

When a person misunderstands us, and is angry, nothing we can say will in any way enlighten him while he is under the influence of emotion. It is best to wait until our would-be antagonist is calm, and then endeavor to communicate. When people cease to communicate with one another, misunderstanding grows. So long as there is communication—not argumentation, but open-minded discussion—there is hope for cultivating understanding and harmony.

It is important never to have a closed mind. Our gurudeva, Paramahansa Yogananda, would not tolerate it in those who sought his training. Whosoever wished to be around him had to keep open-minded, to be a reasonable human being.

In trying to communicate with others, we should always watch our motives. If under the guise of seeking understanding our real intent is to thrust our own ideas down their throats, our motive is impure, and hence wrong. We should always sincerely attempt to understand others, setting aside momentarily our own viewpoint to identify with the other person's thinking. We have to do this if we are to communicate successfully with others. If we are seeking truth, not mere justification of our own convictions, we must be able to let go, for the moment, of what we feel is right, and see the matter through the other person's eyes. Let him express himself. Then, having heard his side, and having impartially analyzed it from his viewpoint, we may present our side. In other words, there must be a fair exchange of ideas. Both parties may then see that they have erred in their thinking, and that truth lies somewhere between their opposite stands.

One trouble with most of us is that we are so busy putting across our own point and trying to convince the other party of it, we don't give him a chance to air his view. When you have difficulties with someone, always give him sufficient respect by allowing him to "get it off his chest." No matter how vicious he is, no matter how emotional, don't interrupt. Let him have his say. Then respond quietly and kindly. Even though he might be saying the most unkind things about you, listen respectfully while inwardly saying to God, "Is this so? I am interested in the truth. If I am this way, You must help me, Lord, to overcome my fault and change myself." But should the person be abusive to the point of forgetting himself, and offend spiritual principles, not mere personal pride and ego, it is our duty to resist, to become like steel. To offend divine principles is to offend God, and we must never be a party to that. Jesus never defended himself, but he was strong in word and deed when righteousness was abused.

Our duty as children of God in this world, then, is to seek understanding: understanding of self, of others, of life, and, above all, of God. This world can be a better place only when understanding reigns in the heart and mind of man. Individuals must learn to get along with one another before nations can ever hope to.

How to Change Others

Self-Realization Fellowship Ashram Center, Hollywood, California, May 19, 1965

The behavior of others should not be allowed to rob us of our peace of mind. It is difficult for anyone to remain mentally calm and hold his tongue when he is irritated by others, but no human being can successfully go through life telling everyone who annoys him how to behave. Unsolicited counsel creates tremendous resentment. One should not try to impose his will or ideas upon those around him unless they have asked for such guidance.

One mistake often made by novices on the spiritual path is that the moment they feel enthusiasm for seeking God, they want to change the whole world. They start a spiritual revolution in the home, with an all-out effort to convert the husband or wife and the children. It is wonderful to have that kind of eagerness, but it almost always arouses antagonism. Paramahansaji used to say to such enthusiasts, "Change yourself first; reform yourself and you will reform thousands." Unless one is seeking guidance, he doesn't want to be told what to do. No one likes to have advice forced upon him. When he is ready for counsel he will ask for it, and he will want it from one with whom he lives, or whom he loves or admires, if he sees a beneficial change has taken place in that person's life. But so long as change is shown only in the form of platitudes or lip service, the doubter will resist.

Be an example of what you want others to be. If you are inclined to lose your temper and fight back or speak harshly; if you scold the children unreasonably; if you are nervous and easily upset, shouting and speaking unkindly—change yourself! That is the best way to change those around you. It is hard to do, but it can be done. One's effort should be directed toward making himself a person who is respected and looked up to; whose word carries weight. He should speak from true wisdom and understanding, never from anger, nervousness, jealousy, or desire to retaliate when hurt.

In India, a very successful manufacturer came to me and said, "I am discouraged and upset; I am having trouble with my wife and with my employees. I am always speaking harsh words to them. What am I to do?"

"Do you want the truth, or do you want me to say what you hope to hear?"

"I want the truth."

"All right," I answered, "you have to begin with yourself. You have a reputation as a tyrant in your home and with your employees. As a result, others obey you because you hold a whip over them rather than because they love or respect you. Consequently you do not get from them the work or cooperation that you could. You should learn to let go; stop being so tense. Every day take a little time to relax; take a little time to think about God. Pretend that in the next instant your whole life will be snuffed away, or pretend you are already dead." (It is a most interesting experiment. Suddenly you find that all your responsibilities are no longer yours. You

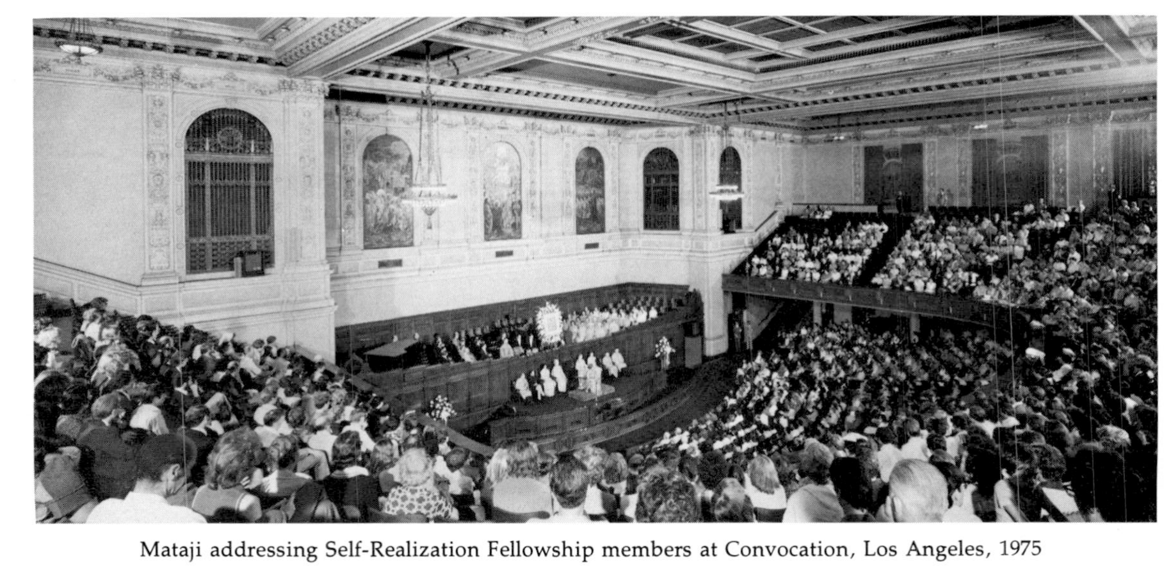

Mataji addressing Self-Realization Fellowship members at Convocation, Los Angeles, 1975

"It is in the consciousness of love divine that Gurudeva Paramahansa Yogananda has drawn all of us together. With the strong but gentle thread of love he has bound us together to form a fragrant garland of devotion, of love, to be offered at the feet of the One Love, the Supreme Beloved of our souls."

Reception for Daya Mata at YSS branch headquarters, Ranchi, India, 1967

"By clinging to the consciousness of God as we pass through all the experiences life brings, we once again behold ourselves, and everyone around us, as a part of the Infinite Whole."

realize how important it is to be more than a little bit concerned about your future with God.)

Then I said to him, "If you wish, while I am here, come every afternoon for *satsanga** and meditate with us." He came every day and we meditated and talked about God.

Two years later, when I was again in India, one of his employees told me, "He is a different man; so much calmer and more patient with us. Because of this there is more peace and harmony among us; we get more done because we are not tense and nervous all the time." This is a wonderful example of what our Guru teaches on this path of Self-Realization Fellowship.

So long as you show nervousness and tension around your husband or wife or children, they will react and behave in a similar way. It can't be otherwise. So if you want a different atmosphere in your home, you have to take the initiative. Do not expect an overnight change in your family. That seldom happens; change is a slow, natural process. And even if it never comes, do not be discouraged or overly concerned. Guruji used to say to us, "God gave every human being a blessed gift: the privacy of his own thoughts. Therein he can live and silently create a companionship and understanding with God that will gradually begin to reflect in his entire life—including his relationships with his family, his community, his world." Even if those around you do not change perceptibly, the change that is wrought within yourself makes you less vulnerable to the misbehavior of others.

* Literally, "fellowship with truth." A *satsanga* is usually an informal gathering of truth-seekers at which the leader speaks extemporaneously about God and other spiritual subjects.

Who Is Responsible for Teenage Behavior?

Often I am approached by parents disconcerted by the ever widening "generation gap" between them and their children. There are many reasons for the problems of today's youth—taken together, these problems constitute a vast and complex subject. Metaphysically, there is the influence of *karma,* of past-life* experiences, in these reincarnated youths, which may be rooted in the tragedies of the wars, riots, and racial abuses of the past thirty years. There is also the effect of mass media. Each segment of society finds every other segment in its own living room on the television screen, and as our *paramguru,*† Swami Sri Yukteswar, said, "Company is stronger than will power."

Consider also the general permissiveness of our society and the lowering of religious and moral standards, as evidenced in publications and entertainment. That which feeds the baser instincts in man is bound to bring out the crude animalistic qualities in him. But setting aside these broader considerations, let me dwell on a few basic truths about the parent-child relationship.

* According to the doctrine of reincarnation set forth in the Hindu scriptures, human beings, deluded by false hopes of happiness and perfection on this earth, become entangled in a web of endless worldly desires. To satisfy them, human beings must seek birth in this world time after time, until they learn life's greatest lesson: that only God can fulfill their desires for happiness.

Rebirth is necessary, also, that the divine law of cause and effect, called *karma*, may be fulfilled. The seeds of man's good and bad deeds must inevitably bear their fruit, whether in this life or another, as St. Paul said (Galatians 6:7): "Be not deceived. God is not mocked: for whatsoever a man soweth, that shall he also reap."

† The guru of one's guru.

We should not wholly blame the teenagers for getting into the difficulties in which so many of them find themselves today. We should look to their parents, and the parents' parents. First and foremost, the parents themselves are frequently undisciplined, and therefore fail to set a good example. I don't mean a holier-than-thou example, but the right kind of example—of understanding, with firmness when firmness is necessary, but never disciplining when their own emotions are out of control. If a parent tries to understand his children he will not hide behind the attitude that "because I am your father (or mother) you have to obey me." That will not work with children.

In addition to giving them love, parents should learn to be companions to their little ones, and this relationship should start at an early age. If parents do not cultivate a rapport with their children when the latter are still very young, there will be no parent-child communication as the youngsters grow older.

Children should not be overindulged with gifts in an attempt to satisfy all their desires. They should have to work for some of the things they want so they will know and appreciate their value. If they do not learn this at home, life will teach it to them sooner or later, perhaps under unfortunate circumstances. Children should be taught to feel a responsibility to earn and merit what they receive.

In some homes the mother does all the cooking, all the dishes, all the housework, and the children are given no duties or responsibilities. This is not right. Children should be expected to perform little chores within their capabilities and age limit. Each should be taught a sense of responsibility and self-respect as a rightful and contributing member of the family.

It is very important that parents understand the child's point of view, that they always try to see things as the child sees them. Then the parents can better help the child to see the matter correctly and in the right perspective. And never, never should the parent scold or spank a child when the parent is himself angry or emotional. The child will not respect or respond to that kind of discipline. He will respect the parent who behaves toward him with wisdom, love, and understanding.

Parents should think clearly and carefully before they lay down the law to their child, and then when they say "No," they must mean it. The child should not be allowed to feel that sooner or later his parents will forget what they said and he will then be able to do what he wants. Children are smarter than you may realize. They should not be given the opportunity to think that if they bide their time long enough one of the parents will relax his insistence on obedience. The child is clever enough to know what he can get away with; it is human nature.

The successful parent will always think first, "Is what I am going to say to my child a mere assertion of my own opinion and authority; or is it right because it is reasonable and just?" Then once having said it, he should make the child obey. A child will come to respect that kind of discipline if at the same time he sees it is meted out with fairness and understanding. His love and respect will make him want to try to please his worthy parent.

Today there is so much defiance in children. It is because they have never been taught that a part of life is learning to respect authority and the rights of others. How many parents, a few years ago, believed in the idea that a child is a young adult who should be allowed complete freedom of will to express himself. Good heavens! Why do you suppose God put parents here on earth? If He hadn't intended that children have the guidance of a mother and father, He would have had the parents lay eggs, so that once the children were hatched the parents could walk away and leave them to their own devices, as the turtle does. God expects parents to assume the responsibility of molding their offspring. Couples who bring a child into this world have no right to fail him.

I believe a child should be encouraged to go to Sunday school, but that he should never be compelled to do so. It is a mistake to try to force a child into any particular religious mold. First he has to have a desire for and an interest in things spiritual. This inclination will be there if from a very early age he is encouraged in cultivating spiritual attitudes: love for God, faith in God, a feeling of companionship with Him. Paramahansaji taught that there should be regular periods when parents and children come together for prayer and meditation. In this way the child begins to relate to God through the parents' example. But family worship should not be too long because children are restless and their minds are not controlled. It is difficult for them to sit long at one time. An excellent practice is to read or tell children stories that will develop in them a sense of morality, faith, right behavior, and love for God. This is the ideal of India. There the earliest instructions that reach the sensitive and receptive ears of the children are the noble and inspiring stories of the scriptures.

Children should never be given the impression that if they do wrong God is going to punish them. They must learn to love God, not to fear Him; to do right because they love Him. They should be taught a little bit about the karmic law: "What you sow in this world, my dears, you will also reap. If you tell lies, then others will be untruthful to you, and they will not trust you. If you steal or take forcibly from others, then others will also take from you. But if you are unselfish, others will be generous to you. If you are loving, others will love you."

It is the duty of parents to open up the minds and hearts of their children and to guide them in the cultivation of the right attitude toward life, toward their emotional problems, and toward sex, when they are old enough. While they are being taught, they should always feel that no matter what they do, their parents will always have an open heart and an understanding mind. A child ought not to feel that he has to go to someone else for the understanding he did not get from his parents.

A wise parent will never act astounded, overcome, dismayed, or shocked by anything his child says to him. The child should always be made to feel, "I can go to my mother and father with anything that is troubling me, because I know I will always receive understanding."

Once a youth came to me and said, "I can't talk to my father or mother. The moment I try to discuss my problems—and they are deep for me—my parents seem not to want to listen; or they scold me, or give me ultimatums. They won't allow me a chance to express myself; so as a result, I've learned to be quiet. I don't talk with them. They don't know these thoughts and these troubles I am having. They are too busy, or they don't want to hear them, or they are too impatient with me."

This is one of the great mistakes parents make; they do not take the time to identify with their children's problems and interests. Instead they reason, "Isn't it enough that I give you a home and see that you have good clothes, that I give you a car on Saturdays and let you go out with this one and that one, and that I give you so many of the things you want, including a vacation trip every year?" No, that is not enough. Those things will never take the place of understanding and companionship.

Every parent wants his children someday to say, "I am thankful for my parents; they were firm with me, but I always knew they loved me and that I could go to them with anything, knowing I would receive understanding, guidance, and patience." But in order to be that kind of mother or father, the parent must also be willing to discipline himself. He has to set the right example, physically, morally, intellectually, and spiritually. He has to cultivate wisdom, patience, and understanding, and he has to exercise perfect self-control whenever he is dealing with his child. Thus will he be able to fulfill the divine responsibility he takes upon himself when he brings a child into this world.

The Divine Meaning Behind Human Relationships

God gave us human relationships in various forms for one reason: we are to learn from one another. Everyone is in a sense our "guru," our teacher. Children teach us, they discipline us; we have to learn endless patience and how to reach out of ourselves, outside our own selfishness and self-interest, in order to help mold their lives correctly. We in turn are their "gurus," for it is our responsibility to guide and train them and give them the best possible start in life.

From all these relationships we acquire an expansion and purification of our love; and I believe that, in the ultimate sense, only love can change others. If you approach a child, or a husband, or anyone, in that consciousness of love and endless understanding no matter what they say or do, no matter how they hurt you, you can't help but win in the end. But you must also have the patience to go on trying.

Set the example in your own life of the qualities you want to bring out in others. "How to live"—that is a great science. Paramahansaji said to us, "When I went to my guru, Swami Sri Yukteswar, he told me, 'Learn to behave.'" And so must you learn to behave in this world: that is the science of religion. When you learn how to behave, you will know what God is, because you will then conduct yourself in such a manner that you will know every moment that you are the soul, not the mortal body or mind. The soul is always drinking deeply of the divine nectar of God's presence. You are not a mortal being, you are a divine being; so learn to behave like one.

That can only be done when a person puts religion into practical, everyday practice, as Self-Realization Fellowship teaches us. Religion isn't something to be gloriously expounded on Sundays and forgotten the rest of the week. Our Guru said to us, "I am not interested in ordinary church followers. If I were, I could have had thousands upon thousands throughout the world. I came to pick out of the crowds of searchers those souls who are deeply and sincerely in earnest about knowing God." He didn't mean that he wanted to make monastics of everyone. He used to say, "Make your heart a hermitage, where you can silently retire to worship God." In that hermitage of your heart put God first. How wonderful it is when He becomes the Beloved of your soul, the Friend of your soul, the Father, the Mother, the Companion, the Guru of your soul. Life becomes rewarding, your relationships with others joyous experiences. You love your children, your husband, your wife, with God's greater love and understanding and compassion. He strengthens the ties between human beings, between human hearts, and frees their earthly relationships from the bonds of selfish attachment that tend to confine and smother love. Nothing suffocates love like possessiveness. "Because you are mine, you have to do this; I have a right to treat you this way." This is often the deathblow to a human relationship.

I feel that before two persons marry, and before they have children, they should be required by law to go to a school where they would learn the art of right behavior. When one is spiritually and psychologically educated to know something about human nature and the art of getting along with others, there is then potential for a happy, harmonious, spiritually progressive family life. The soul flowers in such an enlightened relationship.

Human beings fail in their personal relationships when they cease to have respect for one another; husband for wife, wife for husband, children for parents, and parents for children. Human relationships deteriorate when friendship is lacking in them. Without friendship, the love between husband and wife, children and parents, is soon destroyed. Friendship gives the other person freedom to express himself and his own unique identity.

When there is complete understanding and communication between two souls, there is real friendship and real love. When people learn to keep friendship, respect, and regard in their marital, parental, and other relationships they will never abuse each other, or hurt themselves by such abuse.

You may say, "Yes, it would be ideal if only my husband (or wife, or children) would do it!" Why don't *you* be the one to begin it? Do your part; leave the rest in God's hands.

It always comes back to the same thing: one must begin with himself.

Lessons We Can Learn from Others

Self-Realization Fellowship international headquarters, Los Angeles, California, December 4, 1964

The most spiritually helpful thing we can do for others is to become truly understanding, kind, and loving ourselves. The best way to change others is first to change oneself. As we become more peaceful, calm, and loving, we cannot help but influence similarly those around us.

There are many ways to bring about a spiritual change in oneself. The most important of these is meditation. One must strive to establish a personal relationship with God, so that in one's consciousness the Lord is no longer just a name, or a remote Being, but a loving, tangible reality. In that relationship the devotee enjoys such security, peace, joy, and love that he responds to everything from that inner state of fulfillment.

We react to others, positively or negatively, according to their vibrations. But we should not be content with that human reaction; we are on this earth to realize that all are souls, made in the image of God.

It is very easy to express the best within us when we meet someone toward whom we feel spontaneously drawn. But it is a great truth also that familiarity breeds contempt. When we are with those we love, and who love us, we should never take advantage of them. If love is to be perfect and lasting, it must always be accompanied by respect. Without respect, true love is gradually smothered and destroyed. Respect means always remembering that the other person is a soul, made in the image of the Divine.

When we must be in the company of people toward whom we do not respond positively, what are we to do? Suppose someone is angry or resentful toward you. If you are a person of self-discipline, even-mindedness, and discrimination, you won't add fuel to the fire. You will not lose your own self-control and peace of mind simply because someone else has lost his. I recall an example from one of my early experiences here at Mt. Washington, under the training of my guru, Paramahansa Yogananda.

The furnishings of our rooms in the early days were barely adequate—orange crates to keep our clothing in, a hard wooden bed such as we still use, a straight chair, no rug on the floor, and nothing else. One woman who stayed at Mt. Washington for a short time undertook to refurnish the rooms of the devotees, with the exception of mine. This did not disturb me, because I had not come for material things; I had had them in the world. But Guruji noticed the exclusion; he was always quick to notice any unfairness. Gurudeva never spoke unkindly about anyone, but he told me for my own understanding: "She is jealous of you."

I began to practice at every opportunity what Paramahansaji had taught about how to behave toward those who do not like us: "No matter how they treat you, go on giving them love." I took the attitude that I was not seeking anything from anyone but God and my Guru.

Therefore, this woman could not hurt me. Because I sought nothing from her, no desire of mine could be contradicted by her treatment. I was getting what I was seeking from my beloved God and my Guru. Every time I meditated, I would mentally hold this devotee in the love and spiritual light of God.

One day, some time later, she was experiencing unhappiness and loneliness. Those she had made much of had found it hard to get along with her and had withdrawn from her. We happened to meet in the hall. She spoke to me, and I said something to her that must have been comforting. Later she asked to see me and we talked again. She poured out her heart to me. And finally she said, "When you first came here, I resented you because you were so full of spiritual enthusiasm, which I didn't have. But despite the way I treated you, you have given me understanding and true friendship." Then I realized how people change if you remain always lovingly the same toward them. I have seen this work again and again in my life.

Be Thou of Even Mind

Do not be concerned how people treat you; be concerned only with how you behave. This ideal was taught by Jesus, by Paramahansa Yogananda, and by all the great ones. There is a right way to react in every situation in life, toward those who love us and those who love us not; and this is what Lord Krishna meant when he praised even-mindedness as an essential virtue. "O Arjuna! he who is calm and even-minded during pain and pleasure, he whom these cannot ruffle, he alone is fit to attain Everlastingness!"* He didn't say:

* Bhagavad Gita II:15.

"Be even-minded when people are kind and loving toward you." That is easy to do. He taught that we must be even-minded under all circumstances. When you practice this, you see it brings positive results.

Gurudeva was like a crystal-clear mirror, without blemish. Whoever stood before that mirror saw himself exactly as he was, without any distortion or rationalization; he saw his little ego-self in devastating detail. Paramahansaji knew the weaknesses of every one of us. And he did not avoid his duty to train us! Not that he enjoyed this responsibility—I remember his once saying to me, "I don't like to discipline. In my next life, I will not discipline anyone. But the duty of a guru is to find the flaws in the nature of those who seek his spiritual help, and with the scalpel of his intuitive wisdom to lance those psychological boils so they can heal."

That is how self-discipline works also. It teaches us to use discrimination, which is simply the ability to do what we ought to do, when we ought to do it. But unless and until we know what our weaknesses are, we cannot change them. Even when we know our weaknesses, we often lack a sufficiently strong wish to overcome them. But when we are sincere in our desire for self-improvement we are led to someone, a divine friend such as our Guru, who can point out to us our flaws and help us to correct them. The results of our daily associations with other people can also be illuminating in ferreting out our weak points. You will recognize many of your undesirable traits if you analyze your response to other people and their behavior.

Every human being has attracted to himself every facet of his environment, including the people around him. The resulting experiences are essential to his spiritual growth. The devotee can react positively and benefit from his environment, or he can react negatively and be spoiled by it. We always have that choice, because we have free will. But in the ultimate sense, God has placed each one of us where we are, through the workings of His cosmic laws in response to our own actions.

Find Out What God Expects of You

The way to benefit is to strive to understand what God expects of you in all circumstances. If your environment is such that you are constantly irritated and you react with a desire to retaliate, to fight back, to do harm, and you lose control of yourself, you haven't learned the lesson of that situation. You have to develop, through self-discipline, such control that you are always even-minded. It is not difficult to do if you depend more on God. When you become spiritually strong, so that you are never shaken by people or events, only then will you truly be able to give love and understanding to others, not before.

Guruji used to say, "If you have a fiery temper, bite your tongue, and get away from the person or situation that causes you to lose your temper, until you regain your calmness." Nothing is ever gained by losing one's temper. I have always found that with reason, kindness, and understanding I could reach anyone. But I used to recoil from the temper or fiery speech of others. Guruji saw that sensitivity, and began deliberately to make sharp and cutting remarks to me. Because I had such profound regard for him and his words, I felt deeply wounded. I remember saying to him, "Master, why do you do this?" He explained: "Because you are too sensitive to others. I am not saying you have to be hard, but you do have to be strong. The moment people say anything sharp to you, you recoil, you fold up, and that is a weakness." So he disciplined me just as his guru had disciplined him. Gurudeva was always right. He saw that I didn't need softness; I was already that way. He was trying to give me a spiritual backbone, an unconquerable inner strength.

Some years later he once scolded me very severely before a group of the disciples. It didn't disturb me. I left the room on an errand for him. While I was gone, he turned to the other disciples and said, "You see how she behaves? It has been like that for years. No matter what I say to her or how I say it, she keeps always the same even-mindedness. All of you can learn from her." When the devotees present told me this, years later, such joy and gratitude filled my soul! He couldn't have said anything that would have meant more to me because that was the one thing I had been struggling for, even-mindedness under all conditions. How great is our Guru! My whole being is uplifted when I think on all he did for me. How thankful I am!

I have seen that because of his strict training, it is easier to remain inwardly untouched. You all are getting similar training every day. Human beings and the happenings of daily life are giving it to you, although you don't realize it. Every experience is an opportunity to grow. But instead, how often you react in the wrong way.

Those who want to be successful on the spiritual path have to lift themselves up by their bootstraps and climb above the level of ordinary behavior. If we do not make this effort, we will not grow. When we are angry, vengeful, critical of others; when we find fault with others but excuse ourselves, we are spiritually stagnant. Our duty is to correct ourselves.

Be Anchored in Him Who Is Changeless

It doesn't matter what people say about us, or do to us, if we learn what we should from the experience. We were all born in this world to learn to know ourselves as souls. How are we going to know our true selves, if we don't conquer this little self, this flesh, and this emotional, moody, constantly changing mind? And it can be done, by self-discipline and by practice of deep meditation; by devotion to God, making Him the Polestar of our lives; by fixing the mind on that one Goal. Man's consciousness is always centered in something. It may be sex, money, or possessions. One has to be fixed in something, whether an object, an emotion, or in the soul. Our choice is as simple as that. What is it going to be? Everyone should learn to be anchored in Him who is changeless. That is the wisdom taught by Lord Krishna in the Bhagavad Gita. Become anchored in God and you will find it very easy to cope with life.

The Importance of Loving God

Special annual meeting of Yogoda Satsanga Society of India in Calcutta, September 25, 1961

Beloved ones, I would like to say a few words about that essential ingredient in life which has meant so much to me all through the years: love—divine love, love for God. In this world, love is the one thing that all men are seeking, that every heart is craving. All forms of love—the love between family members, friends, husband and wife, lover and beloved—all come from one common fountainhead, God. The love we receive through all forms of human relationship is but an expression of the Love that is God.

This is why we should seek God. We all want love and joy, and in their purest form these can be found only in Him. But we seek everywhere else first. Only when we have passed through the trials of life, enduring much suffering and sorrow, seeing our dreams burst like bubbles, do we begin to get a little devotion for God. Then we begin to seek Him.

In my relationship with God I like to think of that Divine One in the aspect of Mother.* A father's love is

* The Hindu scriptures teach that God is both immanent and transcendent, personal and impersonal. He may be sought as the Absolute; as one of His manifest qualities, such as love, wisdom, bliss, light; in the form of an *ishta* (deity); or as an ideal being in such form as Father, Mother, or Friend.

often qualified by reason, and by the merit of the child. But the mother's love is unconditional; where her child is concerned, she is all love, compassion, and forgiveness. So, God as Father we conceive as almighty, the Lawmaker and the Judge. But we can approach the Mother aspect as a child, and claim Her love as our own, regardless of our merit.

The principal questions that so many people ask me are how they can bring a response from God, and how they can find peace. The ordinary man is so preoccupied with the worries and responsibilities of his life that he knows no inner peace. And his mind is always so busy with work and with seeking material pleasures that he finds no time for God. Neither God nor peace can be found by one who has not yet learned how to turn his mind to God in deep meditation.

Scientific techniques of meditation, such as the *Kriya Yoga* of Lahiri Mahasaya,* concentrate and still the mind so that it becomes like a calm, clear lake in which the moonèd reflection of God can be seen. In this state of absolute peace, the devotee forgets his delusive identification with the body and mind and realizes: "I am the immortal Self, made in the image of God." The

* Lahiri Mahasaya was the one to whom Mahavatar Babaji revealed the sacred knowledge of *Kriya Yoga*, ordaining him to teach this divine science. When Paramahansa Yoganandaji was but an infant, Lahiri Mahasaya took him on his lap and spiritually baptized him, saying to his mother, "Little mother, thy son will be a yogi. As a spiritual engine, he will carry many souls to God's kingdom." This was later confirmed when Mahavatar Babaji chose Paramahansa Yogananda to spread *Kriya Yoga* in the West and throughout the world, instructing Swami Sri Yukteswar, a God-realized disciple of Lahiri Mahasaya, to spiritually train Yoganandaji for this mission. These four great *avatars* constitute the line of Gurus of Self-Realization Fellowship/Yogoda Satsanga Society of India.

more he experiences of this state of great peace and ecstasy, the more he wants to hold on to it always. As he dives deeper and deeper in meditation, he finds within himself a bottomless sea of peace, divine love, and bliss.

Set Aside Time for God Alone

God has given us twenty-four hours every day. We waste much of this time. Can we not set aside some of it for God alone? We make the excuse that we have so many worries and responsibilities that we have no time for meditation. But what if God says that He has no time for us? In an instant, all our so-called important engagements would be canceled.

It is easy to find God if we seek Him through *bhakti,* devotion. No matter what we are doing, our minds should never wander away from God. Inwardly, talk to Him unceasingly in the language of your heart. Remember, it is His love alone that comes to us through all human forms. So, just as the lover ever thinks of the beloved in the background of his mind, no matter what else he is doing, let us be similarly attentive to God.

Keep your mind focused on the guiding light of the Divine Polestar. When difficulties come, run to the feet of the Divine Beloved. Pray to the Lord: "Give me wisdom to see that this world is only a cosmic drama in which I have a temporary part to play. My Beloved, while I enact my role, teach me to be anchored in Your changeless consciousness as I behold all the sorrows and joys of life."

Guruji wrote: "In waking, eating, working, dreaming, sleeping, serving, meditating, chanting, divinely loving, my soul constantly hums, unheard by any,

'God! God! God!'"* This is the way of the true lover. Be always absorbed in the thought of God: "My Beloved! My Beloved!" And in that consciousness perform all your duties and other activities.

* The complete poem, entitled "God! God! God!" appears on page 220.

Spiritualizing Life

Self-Realization Fellowship international headquarters, Los Angeles, California, May 2, 1963

By adhering to just four principles, the devotee can cope successfully with whatever difficulties he may encounter, whether in his spiritual *sadhana** or in the ordinary affairs of life.

First comes faith in God. In any trial, strive for faith; it is developed by making God the polestar of your life. Pray in meditation, and whenever the problem comes to mind: "My God, You *are*. I know that You will see me through this great trial." God knows your need and nothing is impossible to Him. Faith links your need to His omnipotence.

The second principle is to meditate deeply, and pray for God's guidance and help, as you strive to free yourself from whatever is troubling you. He wants to help you, and when you are receptive, you will be guided by Him.

The third point is surrender. "Lord, let Thy will be done." Surrender to the will of God is essential on the spiritual path. Whatever happens, whether in connection with the body, one's work, or some other interest, pray that God's will be done; because His will is guided by wisdom. We may think that the fulfillment of a par-

* Path of spiritual discipline.

ticular desire is extremely important to our happiness, but if we only ask God to help us carry out our own wishes, we are not yet seeing with the eyes of wisdom. We should let Him do with us what He chooses; it will always be for our highest good. After praying for God to guide us, and striving our very best for the right outcome, we should show God that we accept His will in all things.

The last rule is to relax and let go of the problem. Release it into God's hands. Once you have done your best, refuse to worry about it anymore. It is possible to get so bogged down with work and worries that you can't even sleep. But how relaxed and peaceful the mind becomes when we have placed our burdens on God's shoulders.

These are four ways to help you to maintain inner peace and arrive at a deeper relationship with God. They will also enable you to throw out of your mind anything that is troubling you and preventing you from meditating deeply.

Plunge the Mind into Meditation

When you sit to meditate, forget everything else. So train yourself that when it is time for meditation, nothing can distract you. The ability to concentrate that deeply comes with regular meditation. In our religious communities no one may excuse himself from the daily periods of meditation; regular attendance is an essential rule. And the reason is that unless a devotee can follow this simple requirement he will not have the self-discipline necessary to reach his divine goal.

Throughout the day's activities, be watchful that you do not become lost in the mental restlessness of worldliness. Inwardly take the name of God. Strive to keep your mind busy thinking of God. This practice Paramahansaji called "spiritualizing" thought. It is achieved by guiding your thinking. For example, when you have a few free moments, there is no point in being indolent or dwelling upon negation; why not think of God or inwardly converse with Him? His presence is so peaceful, so wonderful! Once you form the habit, you want always to be in that consciousness.

By spiritualizing thought, one gradually spiritualizes his actions, so that everything he does becomes a form of meditation. One's whole life should be a continuous spiritual experience.

Learn to Draw from a Higher Power

The material-minded man is always thinking in terms of money, home, family, or other responsibilities and interests; and the worries that go with them! The spiritual man may have the same responsibilities, but he meets them by putting his mind on a higher level of thought. By spiritualizing his thinking, he learns to draw from a Higher Power. The time comes when he can go anywhere, mix with anyone, fulfill his responsibilities, and his mind never comes down from the plane of God-awareness. Christ many times associated with "publicans and sinners," in order to help them, but their thinking and actions did not lower his consciousness. Like a divine swan, he moved untouched through the waters of materiality. That is the way Gurudeva trained us to be. Wherever you are, remain always centered within, your mind focused on your polestar: God.

The problems that arise every day give us an opportunity to practice even-mindedness. We should welcome them instead of resisting, becoming upset and irritable, and thinking we are not making progress. Remember this: Often the devotee makes the greatest progress on the spiritual path when he is facing tremendous obstacles, when he is being forced to exercise to the limit his spiritual muscles of inner strength, courage, and positive thinking in order to resist the onslaught of negation, evil, or unkindness. It is not always when things are going smoothly that we are growing. We all naturally treasure those days when things go well; but I have prayed many times to Divine Mother* to test me, because I want my love for Her to be unconditional. I cannot be satisfied with giving Her anything less than perfect love. The devotee of God does not wish to run away from anything. The aspirant might be imperfect in many ways; he lays no claim to any perfection except one: he is striving to perfect his love for God.

Don't pay attention to hardships on the spiritual path; they are nothing, once you have discovered the peace within, when in meditation you forget this body and this world. Such satisfaction, such a sense of joy and the perfection of divine love! This is what God wants all of you to experience. Everyone can realize the divine perfection of God's love if he works for it. Those who experience this love are not exceptions; they had to make the effort, as you must, to love God and to know Him.

That effort is made by striving to keep the mind fixed on God. While facing the daily problems that

* The personal aspect of God, embodying the love and compassionate qualities of a mother. (See page 66 n.)

come, pray within, "Lord, though sometimes my sea is dark and my stars are gone, still through Thy mercy I see the path.* You do whatever You wish with me and my life. All I know is that I love You. Help me to make my love sweeter for You, perfect in every way." What freedom, what joy that brings! Such a relationship with the Divine all can have.

Don't be satisfied with anything less than the love of the Beloved of your souls. His love is all-consuming, all-satisfying. Soul freedom comes when you begin to know yourself as the soul, wed to the one Beloved, the cosmic Divine Lover, God.

The Value of Balanced Living

When you spiritualize your thinking, your mind is always immersed in lofty thoughts. That doesn't mean that your feet are not on the ground, or that you neglect your responsibilities. Gurudeva's training sees to that! I am so grateful for the *sadhana* he has given us, which we can practice in the world and in our ashrams and retreats. If we had all fled to mountain peaks, hoping there to find God, what disappointment might have been our destiny! Most seekers do not have the spiritual strength for that life. A guru who is one with God knows what training each disciple needs, and places him where his spiritual unfoldment can best take place.

Think of the great examples of such divine saints as Teresa of Avila, who was so practical, who founded many convents in spite of great obstacles, and yet was always enraptured with love for God, immersed in His

* From "Polestar of My Life," *Cosmic Chants,* by Paramahansa Yogananda.

love. And think of the struggles and misunderstandings that came to St. Bernadette. The story of her last moments intoxicates me. Despite all the physical and mental sufferings she was passing through, when she perceived the Divine Presence she raised herself up on her bed, whispering, "I love You, I love You, I love You." That to me is perfection. That is the relationship with God I wish for all. And it comes through spiritualizing your thinking by those methods I have explained: faith in God, daily deep prayer and meditation on God, surrender to God's will, and giving your troubles to Him. Isn't that a beautiful philosophy? It is the highest way to live.

After meditating, strive to remain in the state of peace and restfulness felt during meditation. Peace within is the first proof of God's presence. And keeping the mind in that restful state is essential to thinking of God during activity. After meditation, go on recollecting the awareness of God within as long as you can, while you are working, or exercising, or relaxing. The more you do so, the more that state will become natural to you. In truth, it is your natural state of consciousness to live, and move, and have your being in God. But to *realize* this, you must strive to hold on to the joyful, peaceful awareness you experience during meditation.

Gurudeva used to say to us: "Don't let go of it, don't lose it. Rest in that thought, work in that thought, help others in that thought, have all your experiences in life in that peaceful thought of God. Then you are indeed living." Remember that life is a dream. It is not real except as we relate all of our experiences to God. When we meditate deeply we go behind the screen, as Guruji would say, and become aware of the divine Director who is controlling this movie of creation, guiding it and guiding us.

Truth Is Simple

When we brought problems to Paramahansaji there was never a lengthy discussion, just one simple answer: "Keep your mind on God." How grateful to him I am for those words of wisdom, and for the simplicity of the way he taught us to follow the spiritual path. Because God is simple. Life seems complicated because it is not real; only Truth is simple.

When a person builds his life on a lie he spends all his time trying to cover up. He weaves a web around himself and then can't extricate himself. But when a person is always truthful, he is direct; there is no complication to his thinking or his life. It is the same way with God. When an individual sincerely seeks God, he finds just a simple, straight path. It is only when you look outward to the world that you see complication. When you look inward to God you see utter simplicity, divine and joyous simplicity. That's what God is. And that is the way you must make your life. Then you will know Him.

The View of the Wise Toward Life's Experiences

Self-Realization Fellowship international headquarters, Los Angeles, California, March 25, 1971

From among the treasured notes Gyanamata* wrote to me throughout my earlier years in the ashram, I want to share with you some of her wisdom. Gyanamata lived by these four principles she outlined for me, and she counseled and encouraged us to do the same:

> See nothing, look at nothing but your goal,
> ever shining before you.
>
> The things that happen to us do not matter;
> what we become through them does.
>
> Each day, accept everything as coming to you
> from God.
>
> At night, give everything back into His hands.

See nothing, look at nothing but your goal, ever shin-

* Gyanamata (Mother of Wisdom) was one of the first *sannyasinis* of the Self-Realization Fellowship monastic order. Paramahansa Yogananda often extolled her saintly spiritual stature. She entered the ashram in 1932 when she was in her early sixties; Sri Daya Mata had entered the ashram a year earlier, at age seventeen. As one of the younger disciples, whom Paramahansa Yogananda often left in Gyanamata's charge when he was away from Mt. Washington, Sri Daya Mata was helped and inspired by Gyanamata's exemplary life. *(Publisher's Note)*

ing before you. This is a basic principle of the spiritual path, because the search for God is a way of life. It isn't enough to go to church devoutly on Sunday, only to return home and continue to live in a God-forgetful worldly way. We must realize that what we see, what we think, and what we do determine what we are. The deep seeker after God should not concentrate his time and attention upon distractions, on anything that pulls the mind away from God. He should not look at the negative side of life nor become involved in it. Gurudeva Paramahansa Yogananda taught us to avoid those thoughts, activities, and diversions that are incompatible with a sincere desire for God. We ought always to hold before us that ideal.

Those of you who live in the world should not waste time going to cocktail parties, or to movies that do not uplift and inspire, or are downright base in the reactions they arouse. Never do anything that drags the consciousness down from your goal—God. One may think, "Well, I can do as I please today; when I go home tonight I'll have a deep meditation." But you can know for certain that one who reasons thus will not find God in this lifetime.

We should try every day to so conduct ourselves that we always remember our identity with God, for we are His divine children. Guruji often quoted this familiar maxim: "See no evil, hear no evil, speak no evil." Figurines of three monkeys, epitomizing this wisdom, are common in India and also in this country. One monkey has his hands over his eyes, the second monkey covers his ears, and the third his mouth. Let no improper use of the senses defile the God-aspiring consciousness.

The things that happen to us do not matter; what we become through them does. We should never become downcast or discouraged by our mistakes or by the unfortunate things that happen to us as a result of the misbehavior of others. On occasion we have all done things that we were ashamed of later, when we realized our behavior was wrong. But it is equally wrong to allow the memory of those mistakes to poison the rest of our life. We must not allow anything to embitter us, to destroy our faith in ourselves or in our fellow beings, or to fill us with guilt complexes. The right spiritual reaction to all experiences is to determine that we will learn from them and change ourselves for the better.

Recently I came across a letter I had sent to Master when I was a very young disciple. He had evidently scolded me, and I had written to him, "I promise you, Master, I will do the best I can every day to be positive, and not to resist your guidance in thought, word, or action." When one is strong-willed and positive-minded, there is a tendency to want to have his own way. Such a person is sure that he knows best. The divine duty of the guru is to help the disciple to learn how to develop wisdom-guided will. By his discipline Master was helping me to learn from my mistakes.

He used to caution disciples who would not give up egoistic misguided will: "If you keep on like this, Divine Mother will send you away." These words frightened me at first, but soon I recognized that he was merely trying to point out to us the divine law. And now I say the same thing to all of you who seek God on this path. Don't persist in the errors of your ego, but try to conform to the guidance of Guru; otherwise the law of *karma* does cause one to fall away from the spiritual path.

When I tended to judge myself too harshly—and consequently to suffer a great deal—because I felt I was not living up to Gurudeva's expectation one hundred percent, he again gave me the right perspective: "What is past is past. Correct yourself and forget the past. Don't give any more thought to it." Gyanamata is saying the very same thing. The unintentional wrongs you do, or the unpleasant things that happen to you do not matter. What is important is what you become as a result of these experiences. You alone determine your reactions to all of the circumstances that life brings. Will you become an embittered, discouraged, self-pitying human being; or a divinely understanding, compassionate, strong-minded individual, dedicated to God? No one can prevent your success in your search for God, except you yourself.

Each day, accept everything as coming to you from God. This is a vital point. Never think that others are doing you good or ill; see all persons as instruments of God. Be a divine soul, a devotee earnestly seeking God, who sees the hand of God behind everything that happens to him and to others. Know full well that it is God and God alone who silently and lovingly watches over our lives. Each day accept everything as coming to you from the hand of God, and you will begin to realize His constant nearness and blessing.

At night, give everything back into His hands. Never make the excuse that your mind is so filled with thoughts of your work and duties that it is not able to think about God. This is one of the basic problems that everyone on the spiritual path has to overcome, whether he lives in a monastery or in the world. We tend to become so absorbed in our responsibilities that it is difficult at the

Absorbed in deep meditation while ashram residents observe Ram Dhun, twenty-four hours of continual chanting of the Lord's name, Ranchi, India, February 1968

"It is only by learning to still our consciousness, as the great ones have taught, that we are able to perceive within ourselves the presence of the Divine. He has been with us from the beginning of time; He is with us now, and He will be with us through eternity. Hold fast to That which is changeless."

Feeding neighborhood children, most of whom come from impoverished families, Yogoda Math (YSS headquarters), Dakshineswar, India, 1961

"With meditation comes self-forgetfulness, thinking more in terms of one's relationship with God, and of serving God in others."

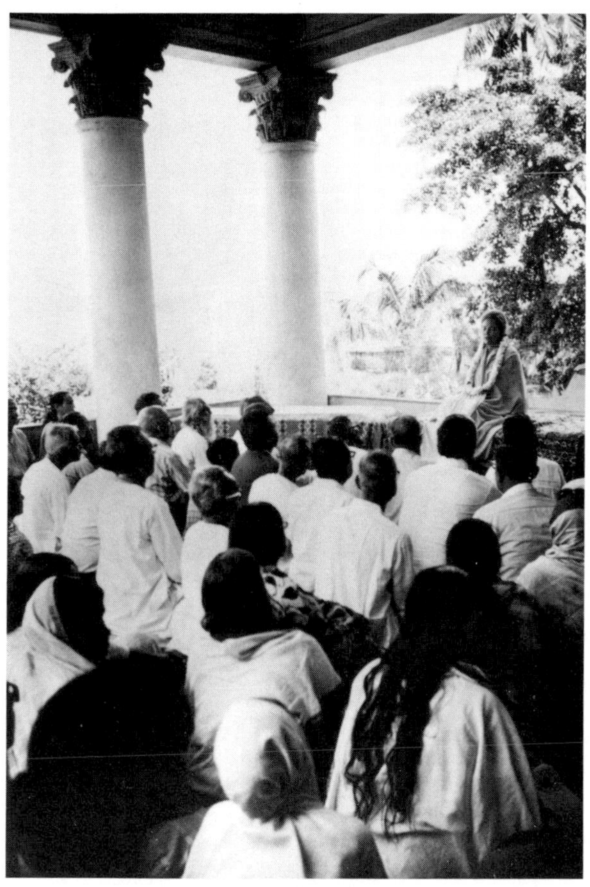

Satsanga at Yogoda Math, by the Ganges at Dakshineswar, India, 1973

"The devotee feels so much a part of God that he relates every experience to God. Whether he is involved in world affairs, busy in his office, or showing love for husband, wife, or children, he realizes it is all God—from God and for God."

Ananda Mata (see page 176 n.), Sri Daya Mata, and Mrinalini Mata (SRF vice-president), Malabar Hill, Bombay, 1973

"One of the great delights of this world consists in never getting too used to anything, so that we can always find something new, inspiring, and thrilling about our life. . . . Practice this ideal of not taking anything or anyone for granted."

time of meditation to mentally throw them off. But we must realize the importance of doing so.

At night, and whenever your time for meditation comes, mentally give everything back into God's hands. You may have been busy with your housework, or with office, factory, or school work, or with financial problems—whatever is involved in your personal responsibilities. These are your duties throughout the day; but at night, when comes the period for meditation, mentally place those responsibilities back in God's care. If you make this mental act every night you will find that it will gradually become much simpler for you to drop everything but God from your consciousness at the time of meditation. Then you will be free to commune with Him.

I urge you to remember these four points, because if you do, you will find them very, very helpful to your spiritual progress. In this life we all have an opportunity to know God; our success depends upon how we react to all of the experiences that come to us.

Thoughts on Right Attitude

Self-Realization Fellowship Ashram Center, Encinitas, California, December 11, 1962

Lord Buddha once said: "The profit of the holy life, O monks, lies not in gains and favors and honor, nor in the fulfillment of morals, nor in the fulfillment of concentration, nor in knowledge and vision; but just this, O monks: the sure, unshakable deliverance of the mind. That is the aim of this holy life. That is its heart. That is its goal."

What is meant by the "unshakable deliverance of the mind"? It means that the mind is always free from the compulsion of habits, emotions, and attachments; and is governed only by wisdom, love, and selflessness. It means that the ego no longer controls you; that you, the soul, operating through the mind, are the master of your fate. The expression of right attitude in all conditions and situations is evidence of that self-mastery.

Right attitude is the way to God. Without it one can never know Him. It is the very foundation of the spiritual life. One must strive constantly toward right attitude, or no amount of speaking of God, no amount of reading scriptures, no amount of years at the feet of a guru, is of any avail.

Implicit in right attitude is humility. You cannot know God without first accepting yourself as the least in His eyes. This does not mean you should go around proclaiming and bemoaning how little you are. No. Humility means that no matter what anyone says or does to you, you remain always the same. When a rose is crushed in the hand, it continues to give off its fragrance. When people crush you in their hands of criticism, in their hands of sharp unkind words, the right attitude is to go on giving sweetness, kind words, kind actions, and—above all—kind thoughts in return. Without kind thoughts, one cannot sincerely express kindness in words or actions.

The trouble with most people is that when they get angry or upset, they don't want to listen to reason, they don't want to understand. When one is blindly convinced that he is right, no amount of explanation, no amount of reason will he accept. He only knows that his own desire has been thwarted, and that's all that matters to him. He "sees red," so to speak. That is the time right attitude should be adopted.

Thy Will Be Done

If anything in this world can make us angry or make us lose control of ourselves, it means simply that we do not have right attitude. If you analyze it, you will find that anger is a result of a desire frustrated. It may well be a noble desire, but still the basic fact is there: anger comes when we are going in a certain direction and then find we have met an obstacle—our desire to go ahead is obstructed. Attitude determines our reaction to this. If our attitude is right, we will, at those times, be able to say, "Lord, not my will, but Thine be done." This brings complete release from the emotion of anger—if we practice it sincerely. Right attitude comes when we work at it steadily; and it always brings peace of mind.

God works through man to accomplish His will in this world. We should strive always to be receptive to Him. This is where right attitude comes in. We are good or poor instruments of God according to the degree of our receptivity, according to the degree of our right attitude. This variation in "degree" is a primary basis of difference in individuals.

Be an Instrument of God

Sri Yukteswarji said to our guru, Paramahansa Yogananda: "Learn to behave." And Gurudeva admonished us: "Strive always toward right attitude." These instructions are one and the same thing. It is by practicing right attitude that we develop receptivity; and receptivity, in turn, enables us to be a channel for God's will. Properly installed electric wires conduct electricity, but of what importance is the conductor if no electricity is present in it? In the same way, our true value lies in being able to serve as a conductor through which God can work His will on earth. It is the duty of each one of us to strive always toward right attitude, that we might have both the receptivity and the humility to be perfect instruments of the Divine.

As we near the Christmas season, perhaps you all feel, as I do, an increased spiritual fervor and joy, and a more intense longing for God. I don't want to waste my time in this life. See how many things constantly drag us down and try to hold us back on the spiritual path! We have to resist them constantly; but not in a nervous, tense way. We should use calm discrimination to clear the path of all mundane distractions that take us away from God, that take us away from the right attitude which gives us God. The secret of the spiritual path lies in right attitude. Once you learn this, seeking God becomes the simplest, most natural thing in the world.

When you meditate, ask God to give you right attitude. I always pray to God and Guru: "I don't care how You discipline me, or what You do with me, but from each experience let me learn right attitude. Let me never resent or resist Your discipline; and no matter what comes, let me never indulge in self-pity, anger, or discouragement." These qualities belong to the nature of an ordinary egoistic human being. We are *not* ordinary human beings. We are souls. We are all children of God. And that is how we should behave. Get the right attitude in your relationship with God, and it will also be right with the world.

Spiritual Opportunity in the New Year

In Self-Realization Fellowship ashrams, resident disciples meditate together on New Year's Eve from eleven thirty to half past twelve, following a tradition set by their guru, Paramahansa Yogananda. Sri Daya Mata led the meditation in 1961 at the international headquarters in Los Angeles. Following are her inspired words to the ashram devotees on that occasion—a loving exhortation to all seekers of God.

Guruji taught that the birth of a new year is an auspicious time for turning the tide of events. It is good therefore on New Year's Eve to introspect, to analyze ourselves and take spiritual inventory. We should consider where we have made progress on the spiritual path, and where we are falling back, and then meditate upon those qualities we hope to make our own in the days to come.

Are we inclined to anger, greed, or envy? Are we distracted by desires that drag our attention away from God—the only Reality? We should not become discouraged by our faults, even if they are many. God loves us in spite of them, and He helps and encourages us no matter what our failings, so long as we are trying to improve. When the devotee stretches forth one hand to God, seeking His help, the Divine Beloved reaches down both His hands to uplift that devotee. So let us ever keep at least one hand outstretched toward the Divine, praying for His guidance. And let us resolve to make a greater effort in this new year to sweep aside everything that would take us away from God.

What is evil and what is good? These are relative terms. What may be good for one person may be evil for another, and what may be manna for one may be another's poison. A great saint of India said that any thought, word, or action that takes the devotee's mind away from God, drawing his consciousness downward into restlessness, despondency, anger, and jealousy is wrong, or evil, for that devotee. We should strive to live in such a way that we think, say, and do only those things that are uplifting to our consciousness.

It is easy to retort harshly to those who speak angrily to us, to feel jealousy when we are neglected or ignored, or to sulk when we feel that others have not given us what we consider our due. But my own experience has been that when we learn to accept everything as coming from the hand of God—when we feel, through deep meditation and constant practice of His presence, that in all life's experiences it is God alone with whom we have to do—it is possible to avoid all the pitfalls on the path to Self-realization.

Each soul is made in the image of God. His qualities of humility, wisdom, love, joy, and bliss are already within us. But the "I," or ego, makes us forget our true nature. We realize it again by dwelling consciously upon our innate divine attributes.

The Light of God Destroys Darkness

All moods and habits that take the mind away from God can be overcome by substituting positive thoughts of cheerfulness, willingness, joy, unselfishness, love, kindness, compassion. As you awaken these qualities within, those other habits of greed, selfishness, anger, hatred, jealousy, unwillingness, passion, will gradually die away. You cannot remove darkness in a room by complaining that you cannot see, or by beating at it with a stick. There is only one way to remove that darkness: let in the light. Similarly, the way to remove ignorance is not by dwelling upon it in self-pity or by berating anyone else for our inner darkness, but by bringing in God's light. Turn on the light of wisdom within, and all the darkness of centuries will vanish.

Devotees who live in the consciousness of God find that they are always centered in Him, that the mind is constantly revolving around some aspect of the Divine: my God, my Father, my Mother, my Child, my Friend, my Beloved, my Love, my Own. The more one strives to hold on to this consciousness, the more quickly he will realize within himself the Divine Image that dwells in every one of us.

Reinforce Your Good Resolutions

Hold a spiritual desire in your heart and deeply pray to God to fulfill it. Pray unceasingly, not for just a few hours or a day, but every day. Even in the midst of activity, let that prayer rotate in the background of your mind. If you have constant faith and zeal to drive that one thought toward fulfillment, you will find that God answers. He never fails His devotees; but you have to be persistent. If at first you do not receive His answer, do not give up; go on trying. Suddenly, when you least expect it, the Divine Beloved will respond to your prayer.

Choose a wrong habit you want to overcome, or a

good habit you want to develop, and make up your mind that throughout this new year you will work every day toward the fulfillment of your goal. Do not make many resolutions and then forget them in a few days, or a few months; decide on one good quality and apply your attention, determination, and zeal until you have established it within yourself.

I remember, many years ago, resolving to struggle for humility in the year that lay ahead. Every day I worked toward that goal: I dwelt upon what humility really is; in my meditations I asked God to give me more humility, and to teach me this quality by whatever means He felt would be most helpful. I struggled in every way, in meditations and in activity, to cultivate that quality. In the same way I have striven on other occasions for devotion to God, for understanding, and other spiritual qualities. These are lifelong endeavors, but the point is, one must make a firm determination and effort even to make a start in acquiring them. This, my dear ones, is the way to fulfill any good desire of your heart. Make up your mind. Apply your will power. Life is passing by, and you want to reap the richest harvest of wisdom, love, understanding, joy, and peace in the season of life yet left to you.

Many seekers say to me, "I don't know if I am going toward God. I feel dry; I don't seem to be making any progress." To such devotees I can only say that there needs to be more effort; there must be greater desire and determination to feel God's presence.

Paramahansaji used to say that the devotee must long for God with the same urgency that the drowning man gasps for breath as he goes down for the third time; with the same yearning that the lover feels when he is parted from his beloved; with the same possessiveness the miser feels for his gold. If the devotee has that degree of zeal, longing, and attachment for God, he will know Him in this life. Let us not be satisfied until we have ignited within ourselves such a spark of divine desire. Resolve in this new year to draw closer to the Lord. Resolve to establish a more deeply binding, a more sweet and loving relationship with God, who is our only true, everlasting Love. When your heart and mind are locked in that divine relationship, all your relationships with others will become purer and sweeter.

Build Your Life on the Rock of Meditation

Make a vow to yourself that, barring illness, you will never forsake your daily practice of meditation. Since I made such a vow at Guruji's suggestion, I have never broken it; and I see the tremendous inner strength it has given me. In addition, have a full day or several hours of silence each week, and have a long meditation during that period. When Guruji told us that, many years ago in Encinitas, I set aside one evening a week for my long meditation. I had many responsibilities to carry; but each Thursday I went to my room at six o'clock, without taking the evening meal, and meditated until midnight. The strength that this habit developed, and the love and devotion I felt for God during those periods of meditation, quickened my spiritual progress. If you would find God, you must make these kinds of resolutions, and not merely pay them lip service, but carry them out faithfully.

During your long period of meditation each week, forget the world and throw all cares out of your mind. Give your problems to God; let Him worry about them for that brief space of six hours. Talk to Him in the language of your heart. Then you will know that you are progressing spiritually. This is the only way you can know—by making greater effort.

Practice the Presence of God

Another way to progress spiritually is through constant practice of the presence of God. Paramahansaji taught that if you would know God you must train your first thoughts in the morning to go toward the Divine; and as you perform your duties throughout the day, think that He is the Doer and you are just the humble instrument. Use your intelligence, willingness, joy, and cheerfulness in serving Him. As the close of the day draws near, let your mind dwell deeper still in God. In these ways go forward with that consciousness of God alone, carrying it through all life's experiences with the greatest of joy in your heart, with the greatest courage and faith and willingness, and above all, with love divine, surrendered at the feet of the One Beloved.

Lastly, let me share with you something I wrote down during one of the New Year's meditations we were blessed to have with the beloved Guru. These words have been helpful to me throughout all these years: "Always remember this: we cannot go against the Divine Will. Each one of us has a different duty in this world, which we cannot escape and which none else can take for us. In fulfilling our duty we must have this attitude: 'O Lord, it is You who are the Doer. Make me Thy willing instrument.' Life is snuffed out in a second. How can we possibly think that we are the doers in this world? The Gita says, 'Forsaking all other *dharmas* (duties) remember Me alone; I will free thee from all sins (accruing from nonperformance of those lesser duties).'*

Just Remember to Do the Best You Can Every Day

"All you have to remember in this life is to do the best you can, every moment, every day. God wants continuity of effort from you. He does not want you to become discouraged and give up and run away. Remember that in the midst of all your activities, and throughout all your trials and tests, God is ever with you. Jesus said to St. Anthony, who spent over sixty years in the desert praying to Christ: 'Anthony, though you were suffering, I was with you all the time.'" Let us remember this assurance whenever we face discouraging circumstances.

Duality is the nature of this world. Never dwell upon the negative side. We must learn to take the good and the bad with strong faith in God. We must realize, as Guruji taught, that the trials we meet in life are but the shadow of God's hand outstretched in blessing. Learn to look upon everything in life with one consciousness: "Lord, You are the Doer. From Your hand I receive the gentle caress and also the slap, because You know what is best for me. You love me through those who are my friends and You discipline me through those who think themselves my enemies."

In this consciousness let us face the new year with courage, faith, strength, willingness to do whatever is placed before us, and, above all, with a constant yearning to feel the love of God. He has not withdrawn Himself from us; we have withdrawn our consciousness

* Bhagavad Gita XVIII:66.

from Him, by running after the things of this world, by overindulging our senses and emotions. It is only by learning to still our consciousness, as the great ones have taught, that we are able to perceive within ourselves the presence of the Divine.* He has been with us from the beginning of time; He is with us now, and He will be with us through eternity. Hold fast to That which is changeless.

My Prayer for You

My prayer for each one of you in this new year is that you may fulfill your highest and noblest aims on the spiritual path. You who seek love divine, may you find it; you who seek understanding, look not for it in human relationships but from Him who is the Fountain of Understanding; you who seek strength, courage, or humility, may you go to the one great Teacher who can help you acquire these qualities, who can awaken the sleeping divinity within you, that you may behold yourselves as true children of God. In memory I hear our blessed Guruji's urging at the new year: "Wake, sleep no more! Wake, sleep no more! Wake, sleep no more!"

The way to peace, joy, happiness, and love divine is to keep your consciousness centered on and at rest in God. Concentrate upon one idea: God alone. "Thou art my Polestar; in Thee I live, move, breathe, and have my being. I seek naught else but to love Thee and to serve Thee." Make this your constant prayer in the new year.

Concentrate night and day on God, and become drunk with His love. He alone is real. In His love lies

* "Be still, and know that I am God" (Psalms 46:10).

wisdom, humility, joy, compassion, understanding, and fulfillment. May each one of us seek that love more earnestly.

Meditate more deeply and strive to serve God with greater willingness, with greater conscientiousness and concentration. It isn't enough just to serve; consider it a great privilege, and serve with zeal, with joy, and with love in the heart. Singing songs of devotion to God, may we carry that joyous consciousness throughout all the days of the new year, that we may close the year as we have begun, thinking only of the One.

The Secret of Forgiving

Self-Realization Fellowship international headquarters, Los Angeles, California, March 24, 1969

Once more the blessed time of Easter is upon us. The holy seasons of the year play a perceptibly uplifting part in my own consciousness, and my prayer is that they similarly inspire yours. When we come to this time of remembrance of Jesus Christ's supreme sacrifice for mankind, I think of Gurudeva Paramahansa Yogananda's oft-repeated declaration that Christ performed his greatest miracle on the Cross. With every right to curse and condemn his betrayer, and the others who had wrongly judged him, and with all power at his command to destroy his enemies, Jesus did not use that power, nor did he feel any enmity. Rather, he showed the world the divine way to conquer evil—the way that alone can resurrect man's soul from dark ignorance into the light of eternal wisdom, eternal communion with God. That way was immortalized in Christ's simple words of love: "Father, forgive them; for they know not what they do."*

This is an extremely important message for mankind even today, a message that each one of us should apply in our lives if we would keep the light of divine love in our hearts and in this world. It is essential to rid

* Luke 23:34.

the heart and mind of all bitterness and resentment; such feelings don't belong there.

When someone has acted unkindly against us, why do we feel we have to do something about it? Why can't we just leave it in God's hands? I believe in this. Cannot we, too, say: "Father, forgive them; for they know not what they do"? knowing full well that the divine law, the divine love, will solve that problem for us. In countless ways this law has worked for me throughout my life; it will work also for you, and for all mankind.

The trouble is with *us.* We cannot let go of our mean and hateful thoughts, of our vengeful, angry, envious feelings. Because we cannot let go of the hand of Satan—of delusion, and that is all these wrong thoughts and feelings really are—we are unable to grasp the hand of the Divine.

Let us try to resurrect our consciousness from the dark sepulcher of hatred, anger, and meanness. You know what meanness is: the desire to hurt another person. All of us probably have hurt others unconsciously at times. We should sincerely ask anyone whom we may thus have hurt to forgive us. And never should we knowingly lift our hand, even in thought, against another human being. If we were to do so, the first to suffer would be ourselves; because in that moment we would lose the inner awareness of God.

Seek Realization of the Soul, Repository of Love

There is but one desire in my soul for you: because of the joy, the sense of peace and security, and the great love that I find in my own soul, I crave to see each one of you bathed in that divine consciousness. True, it is very difficult to achieve that consciousness, and very difficult to hold on to it. My duty, therefore, to those of you who are striving to change your lives in a divine way, is to remind you when you stray from the Goal, and to urge you to follow ever more deeply, ever more sincerely, ever more devotionally in the footsteps of our Guru.

Gurudeva was the very embodiment of kindness, love, forgiveness, and compassion. There was not one mean or selfish streak in him; yet some misunderstood him, even as there were those who misunderstood Christ. When one has habituated himself to darkness, his eyes cannot stand the light; it is blinding. So when anyone turns away from the light of understanding and right behavior, and steeps himself in the darkness of self-pity and self-interest and self-concerns, he resents anyone or anything that reflects that light. If he were receptive to it, he would find that it brightens all the corners of his consciousness and of his life, and gives him the very things he craves, but has not applied the right principles to achieve.

So, in this spring season of resurrection, let us with renewed fervor cry in our souls for God. I do—I want Him desperately every moment of my life. Sometimes I awaken in the middle of night; there is no desire to sleep, only to spend every possible moment talking to God. That to me is reality; and because I find my pleasure, my peace, my joy, in the communion with Him, I want it for every one of you.

My suffering comes when I see those who blindly cling to their faults and weaknesses, and do not let go and let God take charge of their lives. That you must do, if you would achieve Self-realization. Trust more in God, believe more in God, accept God; have faith in

Him who can right every wrong that has been done to you. You don't have to defend yourself; let God be your defender.

When people misunderstand me, my concern is not that they be perfectly attuned with Daya Ma, but with God. At such times I pray urgently to Divine Mother: "Bless them, bless them! Awaken their consciousness in You, let them look only to You, let them cling to You!" In that prayer lies my joy, and peace of mind about my relationship with those souls. Our Gurudeva used to say: "I cannot be content until I see that every one of you—every one!—is racing toward the feet of my Divine Mother." That is also my own humble and earnest wish; because, as he also said: "Always remember, nothing can ever touch you if you inwardly love God." For this reason every one of us should be inwardly in love with God. Then His love—so intoxicating and all-consuming—completely erases any trace of worldliness, so that no matter what anyone may do to us, we are inwardly undisturbed, remaining always in the same consciousness of one divine love toward all.

The mind has tremendous power, to do good or to do evil; and in these days of so much unrest, let us all join in deeply praying for mankind. It is essential that while we as individuals are striving to achieve some degree of realization, some degree of safety in the thought of God, we pray also for this suffering world—pray that man learn how to resolve all his problems, with God, not Satan, as his guide; clinging not to the evil force, but to God, and God alone.

A Time for Prayer, a Time for Surrender

Self-Realization Fellowship international headquarters, Los Angeles, California, May 19, 1966

Sri Daya Mata's discourse was in response to the question: When in need of physical healing, which method is preferable: the practice of surrender? or prayer and affirmation?

During my many years with Paramahansa Yogananda, my gurudeva, I saw that he never prayed for himself. In fact, he once said: "I cannot pray for myself. I have given my life wholly to God, to do with as He will." Guru's life was an example of surrender.

In the highest sense, if we believe in God and have faith in Him, there is no reason to ask Him for anything. He knows our needs better than we, with our limited human understanding. To pray for oneself, then, is a contradiction of our faith in God.

At times, because Paramahansaji took upon himself the evil *karma** of others in order to free them from much suffering, his own body suffered instead. We used to plead with him, "Master, why don't you pray for healing?"

"How can I pray for myself?" he would answer. "I have never prayed for my body. I have given it to God. What He will do with it, He will do. It is all the same to

* Good or bad effects of past good or bad actions. (See page 50 n.)

me." Gurudeva was wholly content in the consciousness of God. When a devotee reaches the state of consciousness wherein he is perfectly anchored in God, as was Paramahansaji, the condition of the body makes no difference. One who prays for his body is still attached to it.

But to pray for others is right and good. Then you are asking, above all, that they may be receptive to God, and thus receive physical, mental, or spiritual help direct from the Divine Physician. This is the basis of all prayer. God's blessing is ever present; receptivity is often lacking. Prayer heightens receptivity. If one's faith is not perfect, prayer for oneself or others is essential to help strengthen faith and open the door to God's ever present help.*

Informal Conversation with God—the Most Natural Prayer

I don't even like to use the word *prayer,* which seems to suggest a formal, one-sided appeal to God. To me, conversation with God, talking to Him as to a near and dear friend, is a more natural, personal, and effective form of prayer. When I hear about the tragedies of war and other sufferings of humanity, or when anyone writes to me and asks for help, I immediately talk it

*Prayers for healing of physical disease, mental inharmony, and spiritual ignorance are offered daily by the Self-Realization Fellowship Prayer Council, composed of renunciants of the SRF Order. Prayers for oneself or one's loved ones may be requested by writing or telephoning Self-Realization Fellowship, Los Angeles. This mission of prayer is supported by the Self-Realization Fellowship Worldwide Prayer Circle, consisting of SRF members and friends around the world, which regularly offers prayers for world peace and the well-being of all mankind. A booklet describing the work of the Worldwide Prayer Circle is available on request.

over with God, conversing with Him in the silent sanctuary of my soul.

If we were in tune and communing with God every moment, where would be the need to pray or ask for anything? We would have such a perfect sense of well-being, of complete confidence in our dependence upon Him, that we would feel a constant inner assurance: "He knows what He is doing with me. I cannot always understand His way, but I am content in the realization that He knows what is best." That is surrender.

Perfect love for God presupposes perfect confidence in God's will in all things. Therefore to pray for oneself would be an imperfection in our devotion to God. When we love someone very deeply, unconditionally, with implicit trust in his love for us, we do not care what he does with us. The same ideal applies to our love for God: we should give life, heart, and mind so completely to Him that no matter what comes it is all the same; the consciousness remains unperturbed, unruffled. He who has that consciousness has his mind so riveted on God, and his being so engulfed in blissful awareness of Him that when a crisis comes, what happens to the temporal body is of no importance. I believe in this attitude of utter dependence upon God.

Surrender does not spare a person from suffering. I remember what Paramahansaji said one evening: "I have experienced pains in this body for years. But how strange it is: on one side Divine Mother is causing the suffering, and on the other She is looking after this body through all of you." His was a complete identification of self with God. In the realization of himself as the soul he was able to stand aside and see that God alone was permitting his body to suffer, and that it was the Divine who at the same time was sustaining his form, and giving it the necessary care.

This surrender is not a depressing state of resignation to sorrow, in which one glorifies suffering as a virtue by praying for it to come to him. The pious devotee who asks God to visit upon him all the sufferings of the world, and who dwells on suffering as a means of pleasing God, is taking a rather negative approach to surrender. I believe in a positive approach: "I am the soul; my nature is blissful, powerful, and perfect. I will take care of this body, but I will not become attached to it, nor lament about any imperfection that develops in it." If one has a headache, it is not wrong to acknowledge the fact and to take whatever logical remedy is available to him; but his consciousness should dwell on the truth that his real nature is separate, untouched by the discomforts of the body form he is wearing.

The Body Is Just a Cloak over the Soul

The body is indeed no more than a cloak over the soul. If a person's overcoat becomes ragged and torn, he does not ordinarily grieve over it; he repairs it, or replaces it with another. Never allow the consciousness to become identified with the bodily coat that the soul is temporarily wearing.

Persons who do not understand the ways of God often have the notion that spiritual perfection means perfection of the body too—that the body of a person who is in tune with God will not be subject to physical disease. Nonsense! One who persists in this idea is himself attached to the physical form; the body is too important to him. I am not saying that one should not give the body reasonable care. Sri Yukteswarji said, "Why not throw the dog a bone?"* Give the body what it needs and then forget it. And Christ said, "Take no thought for your life, what ye shall eat; neither for the body, what ye shall put on. . . . Your father knoweth that ye have need of these things."†

The point is, no mortal man will be permitted to live in his physical form eternally, no matter how well he cares for his body. So why concentrate so much attention on something temporal? To be preoccupied with the care of the body to the exclusion of, or in preference to, the nurture of the soul, is a spiritual error. God allows disease and imperfection to visit the body to awaken us—through suffering, if need be—to the realization that as His children we are not this mortal body, and that this world is not our home. We are the immortal soul and our home is in God.

In stressing the virtue of surrender, we ought not to ignore the place and value of prayer and affirmation. The ideal surrender demonstrated by Paramahansa Yogananda would be high aspiration indeed for the ordinary being, because it is based on perfect spiritual understanding of, and attunement to, the will of God. Such a devotee knows when and how to resist his problems and when to resign himself to suffer them.

"God Helps Those Who Help Themselves"

Jesus had the power to deliver himself from the hands of those who would crucify him: "Thinkest thou that I cannot now pray to my Father, and He shall presently give me more than twelve legions of angels?"‡ But

* *Autobiography of a Yogi,* chapter 12.

† Luke 12:22,30. ‡ Matthew 26:53.

he prayed: "Father, if Thou be willing, remove this cup from me: nevertheless, not my will, but thine, be done."* For one who does not feel this attunement in any given situation, prayer and affirmation are not only beneficial, but also advisable. They help to make the mind and consciousness receptive to the blessings and guidance of God, strengthening faith and stirring the will, which in turn rouses the healing life force. Prayer and affirmation thereby put into operation another cosmic law: "God helps those who help themselves."

The Magnetic Power of Affirmation

Everyone should practice affirmation. To me, two of the most helpful affirmations are: "Lord, not my will, but only Thy will be done through me"; and "Lord, Thou art the Doer, not I."

The world is created on the principle of one particle revolving around another—an electron circling a proton—producing a creative force. Affirmation applies the same principle. Concentrated will power revolving around an idea creates a powerful magnetic force. When an affirmation such as "Lord, Thou art mine; I am Thine," or "Lord, Thou art in his body; he is well," is repeated over and over with increasing force of powerful thought, it brings into existence the very thing being affirmed.

This principle can operate to produce a negative result as well, if concentrated will is repeatedly revolved around a negative thought. By negative thinking one can seriously harm himself or others. For what one sows in this world he also reaps; what thoughts he

* Luke 22:42.

throws out into the ether return to him. That is why Paramahansaji used to say, "Watch your thinking. Know without any doubt that the seeds you sow will one day be reaped by you." Therein lies the importance of positive thinking, right thinking, for the good of oneself and others.

Thought—the Most Potent Force in the World

Thought is the most potent force in the world. Out of the thought of God has come all creation. Nothing can exist without Him. Because we are made in His image, His invincible might resides within each one of us; our thought and consciousness are part of the divine intelligence and consciousness of God. It is not something we have to acquire, but we do have to learn how to tap our inner source of power before we can manifest it.

When you are affirming healing for yourself or others, visualize the tremendous force of God's healing power as a white light surrounding you or the person for whom you are praying. Feel that it is melting away all illness and imperfection. Every uplifting thought we think, every prayer we utter, every good action we perform, is impregnated with God's power. We can manifest this power in greater and greater ways as our faith becomes stronger and our love for God becomes deeper.

Know for certain that if it is ultimately for the highest good, cosmic law and even the will of God can be influenced by the power of prayer and affirmation, when one's thought is strong and faith is perfect. When one has forcefully prayed and positively affirmed healing, with faith and devotion, but the end result is contrary, then comes the time to surrender in inner peace to the higher wisdom of God. But until He has made His final pronouncement, He expects man to use his God-given power, will, and strength to resist all imperfection in this world of change and relativity.

Man's Need for God

Self-Realization Fellowship international headquarters, Los Angeles, California, March 24, 1969

In the world, as in the ashram, the most satisfying life that man can have lies in following the inner spiritual path. When he has God, his heart will not crave anything else. All he has ever sought or longed for, he will find in the complete contentment and satisfaction he enjoys in God. Such a man has only one prayer: that he be deluded no more by this world. Having found God-communion, the opening through which he can escape from the little prison cell of body- and ego-consciousness into soul freedom, he doesn't want ever to be confined again.

This understanding of the imprisoning nature of the ego develops according to the degree to which we surrender that ego, with all its limitations and selfishness, to God. It is impossible for Him to enter into the consciousness of the man who is constantly thinking, "I, I, I." In one who is wholly absorbed in "I" there is no place for "Thou." The first goal to strive for is to remove that "I." It isn't simple, but it becomes easier if one develops a deep yearning for God.

Very often, that yearning for Him comes through suffering. However, I do not regard suffering as essential on the spiritual path. Many interpretations of Jesus' life and teachings dwell on the virtue of sorrow and suffering. This concept is very depressing. Even as a young girl, I rejected it as it was then presented to me; I could not imagine anyone's voluntarily and joyously seeking sorrow or suffering. It is not a realistic or practical approach to God, because those negative states are not natural to the soul. I would never have taken up Yoga had I thought it a path of sorrow! I believed that seeking God ought to bring an end to all pain and unhappiness. Now, after some thirty-odd years on this spiritual path, I am convinced beyond any doubt that finding God and communing with Him does indeed put an end to human misery.

This is not to say that the spiritual aspirant doesn't pass through certain phases of difficulty. It is an unrealistic notion that merely because we pursue God, He ought to remove all obstacles from our path. He certainly could do it; but if He did, whence would come man's strength? A muscle is made strong by use. An inactive arm, hanging limply at one's side, gradually becomes weak and shriveled. So it is with man. If his muscles of faith, dedication, compassion, patience, devotion, loyalty, perseverance—all those undeveloped qualities that lie deep within his soul—are not called upon and exercised during his *sadhana* or spiritual search, he will never change and overcome his human weaknesses and limitations.

God and Man Seek Unconditional Love

God is very patient with His children; He loves us unconditionally. And isn't this the kind of love we crave from Him? We do not want from God a love so insubstantial that if we do something wrong, or are not always able to live up to our highest ideals, He forsakes us. Nor should our love for God be so fragile that if we mistakenly think He has forsaken us, we in turn forsake Him. That kind of love has no meaning. We want love that is unconditional and unending. And if we want it for ourselves, it would seem we ought to be willing to give that kind of love to God, and to strive to give it also to others in this world.

I know full well, no doubt from many past lives and experiences, that no human being can give me what I seek. All the adoration, glory, praise, or love that any human being could give me cannot be enough. God alone can satisfy my soul. Only He can satisfy fully the deep cravings of every one of us.

Hold Fast to God; He Can Help You

We should have faith that whatever be the experiences that come to us, they bear the will and blessing of God. Their purpose is not to punish, but to strengthen us and to prove our love. The One who is ever guiding our lives is God. To the degree that you hold fast to the hand of God, He can help you. Withdraw your hand because of resentment, or because your faith has been weakened by feelings that you are not getting what the world would call a fair deal, and know for certain that you are withdrawing from the very Source of all you are seeking. This great truth is a repeatedly demonstrated fact of life.

Remember that we get in this world exactly what we have given out. It isn't God who punishes us; we create the causes of our painful experiences by our wrong actions of this and past lives. The cause is equal to the effect, and the effect is equal to the cause. Never doubt it for a moment. Strive always to create the cause that will manifest the desired effect. The greatest cause we can set into motion is an active, conscious, ever-increasing love for God. He alone can bring unto every devotee the total fulfillment of all his desires. We ought never to lose sight of this truth.

Pleasing God Should Be Our Motive in Life

Words of devotion for God have very little meaning in the ultimate sense. The only way we can really express what we feel for God is by our actions. Perhaps this explains why the Bible says that by a man's work you shall know him.* It matters little if no one evidences any appreciation of what we do. We should never feel discontented, even if after great effort to be good, and to do good, no one seems to care or appreciate it. We are on earth to work not for man, but for God. Every act should be performed as an offering of devotion to be laid reverently at His feet. It is with God we have to do, every moment of our lives, and in everything we do. He is the Living Force that is guiding us, sustaining us. He alone is ever with us and conscious of our every thought. This is why it is important that our thoughts be always the highest and noblest. Our motivation should be to please Him. In pleasing God we can hope that our life and our service may also be pleasing to His children.

Misunderstanding, and the pain that comes therefrom, does not arise in those whose hearts are pure. The heart will be right only if we do not lose sight of the Goal—God. The devotee cannot lose his way if he re-

* "By their fruits ye shall know them. Not every one that saith unto me, Lord, Lord, shall enter into the kingdom of heaven; but he that doeth the will of my Father which is in heaven" (Matthew 7:20–21).

members to follow the steps that lead to the Goal: constant yearning for God, which comes from practicing His presence and talking to Him; daily meditation, even when there is no desire to meditate; and giving wholeheartedly of one's life and service to God in a spirit of dedication.

God doesn't need us, but we desperately need God. We need Truth. We need to catch hold of the Reality in this great ocean of unreality, and cling to that raft of Reality until we reach safely the shores of infinite, eternal awareness of God.

How to Find Favor with God

Satsanga with center leaders who attended Self-Realization Fellowship Fiftieth Anniversary World Convocation. Satsanga was held at SRF international headquarters, Los Angeles, California, July 13, 1970.

In his teachings Paramahansa Yogananda stressed primarily the importance of diving deep into the sea of meditation to find the pearls of God's wisdom, peace, love, and joy. To hold on to the treasure, Guruji told us, the devotee must live and move and have his being in silence. We practice this in the ashram. You should not assume from this that we spend all our time sitting quietly in meditation; we are very busy here. But we learn to live more within ourselves; we learn not to expend time and energy in useless idle talk. Guruji would sometimes say, "When you shake a pitcher that is only half filled with water, the sloshing of the water makes a loud, hollow sound; but when the pitcher is filled to the top it produces no sound when agitated. That is the way man must be—brimming with the waters of God-consciousness." When the pitcher of the mind is filled with divine thoughts, one has little wish to speak. He would rather be a silent observer, inwardly absorbing that which is good and beautiful around him, and remaining aloof from disturbing and distracting trivialities.

At one of the Yogoda Satsanga schools, Ranchi, India, 1972

"Children teach us, they discipline us; we have to learn endless patience and how to reach out of ourselves, outside of our own selfishness and self-interest, in order to help mold their lives correctly."

Banaras, 1961

"We can make life ever newly interesting, completely fascinating, so that we become entranced with everything in the Lord's creation. How? Avoid looking only to the external; see the Divine Hand behind everything."

Conducting *sannyas* (monastic vow) ceremony for SRF-YSS monks, Ranchi, India, 1968

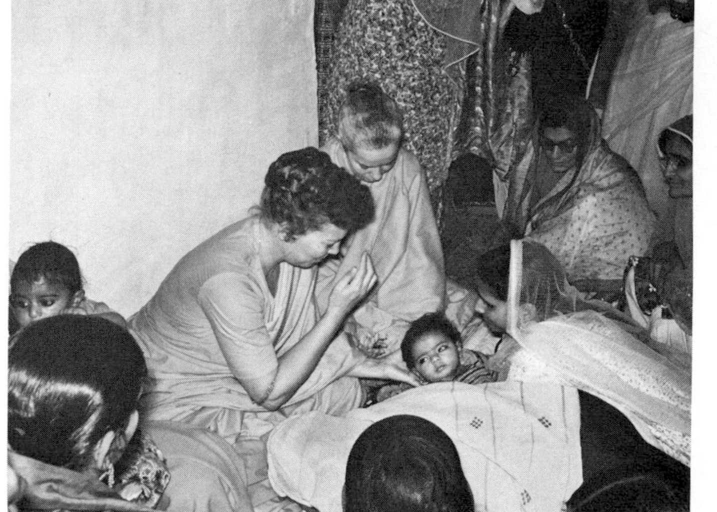

A mother brings her child to Mataji to be blessed, India, 1961.

"Whenever I would read about ideal love between friends, or parents and children, or husbands and wives, I would think: 'Beloved God, if these human relationships can be so beautiful, how much more beautiful

This state is not absentmindedness. No one around Guruji was allowed to be inattentive; he taught us to be ever alert. But whenever our minds had a tendency to become restless or too extroverted, Paramahansaji would recall us to our high goal, saying, "Keep your mind fixed in God."

How many times, after talking with Guru about some problem, I wrote in my diary: "Master said, 'Just give it to God; everything depends upon Him.'" Paramahansaji did not mean that to accomplish one's objectives in this world all one has to do is to sit and pray, and everything will come to him. Suppose we told the scientist, the businessman, or the housewife: "Just sit and pray; God will do your work for you"?

Guruji was always practical-minded; we learned that God helps him who helps himself. The Creator has endowed each person with a spark of His divine intelligence, and we are expected to develop our potential by using that intelligence. While performing our duties, we ought constantly to pray inwardly: "Lord, I will reason, I will will, I will act; but guide Thou my reason, will, and activity to the right thing that I should do in everything." It *works!* I know the effectiveness of this prayer, because this is how the work of Self-Realization Fellowship has been carried on through all these years.

God Is the Easiest to Know

Some seekers complain that it is difficult to know God. Yet He is the easiest to know; because He is not apart from us, He has never been away from us. If He were, we would not be here; we would not even *be.* God has not separated Himself from us; man has separated himself from God. When our thoughts are turned outward, engrossed in the multiplicity of the finite world, we disunite ourselves from Him. This is the simple truth.

How to reassociate our consciousness with God? Upon awakening in the morning, do not think first of work; make it a practice to rise a few minutes earlier than has been your custom, so that before you begin the day's duties you can spend fifteen minutes, or half an hour, in meditation and communion with God. During that period, forget time and your worldly responsibilities; if there is a sense of urgency to finish the meditation, you will not have the receptivity necessary to feel God's presence. During meditation, let go of all extraneous thoughts; think only of God. Talk to Him in the language of your heart. After meditation, carry into all of your activities, to the best of your ability, the meditative peace you have gathered in your heart.

If Miracles Are Your Goal, God Withholds Himself

Eventually, often when you least expect it, you will see some sign of God's sweet response. This is the way one grows in divine consciousness. It requires daily application. That consciousness doesn't come suddenly, with the Divine appearing out of the clouds and writing in letters of gold for you. Don't look for such miracles, for so long as you do, God will withhold Himself. That is His way.

When you are hoping for miracles, it is not God that you desire; you only want Him to prove Himself to you. This He will not do. Give Him your heart sincerely, trust in Him wholeheartedly, unconditionally; then He will give Himself to you. Never will He come so long as you are looking only for His miracles.

Phenomenal experiences are not necessarily evidence of spiritual progress. The deeply sincere devotee is inclined to pray to the Lord not to send him such experiences, because he knows they can be a real distraction from his true goal—God. Spiritual phenomena do not stimulate the devotee's love for God, but rather the desire for Him to prove Himself repeatedly. Many noble souls have fallen from their lofty state because in looking for miracles they lost sight of the Lord. If Paramahansaji saw a devotee going thus astray, he would caution, "That way will lead to delusion. Long for God and love Him for His sake alone. Then He will respond to you." It has been so in my own life. I have prayed to the Divine: "I want nothing from You, Lord; I need no proof. But I do ask of You one miracle: that no matter what comes in my life—no matter what kinds of responsibilities or trials I bear—promise me that I shall never lose my yearning for You. If that longing leaves me, I cannot live." To yearn always for God is my desire, because in that yearning He is constantly in my heart. This is the way the devotee feels.

The Insight That Lifts the Veils of Nature

We can make life ever newly interesting, completely fascinating, so that we become entranced with everything in the Lord's creation. How? Avoid looking only to the external; see the Divine Hand behind everything. Behold the flowers; how fascinating is their beauty, how marvelous that out of tiny seeds, so many of which look alike, such multifarious patterns of beauty have emerged. The wonder of it is intoxicating.

The majority of mankind live superficial lives,

never thinking deeply about anything, looking always for new sensual thrills. The result is that life becomes jaded and empty. This spiritual malaise is widespread in the world today.

Paramahansa Yogananda taught us to appreciate even a grain of sand—no two are alike—and to notice the flowers, the trees, and to value the beauty in them. We learned from him to hold in highest regard all God's creations, seeing their Creator behind the material forms. When one learns to live in that spirit, he sees heretofore hidden beauties in nature—he beholds God's handwriting across the vast blue sky. This insight that lifts the veils of nature to reveal God comes by continually practicing the presence of God. Everything in life, the multitudes, the many, can ultimately be reduced to One. God is the great Common Denominator of all creation, of all mankind. Keep Him always in your thoughts, no matter what you are doing. This is the meaning of *karma yoga* as well as *bhakti yoga*.*

The Requirements of a True Karma Yogi

Karma means "action"; *karma yoga* is the path of uniting the little self with God through selfless activity. If one would know God in this world, he must strive always to do that which is right, that which is good, that which is constructive; and as Paramahansaji said, "Always think that what you are doing, you are doing for God."

Each one has his duties to perform, duties given to him by God and by karmic law through the effects of

* *Bhakti Yoga* is the spiritual approach to God that stresses all-surrendering love as the principal means for communion and union with God.

his past actions. He must fulfill those responsibilities and not shirk them, doing his best while having full faith in God's wisdom and guidance. When one acts for himself, he is identified with his own little ego. But when he surrenders everything to God, he realizes his innate oneness with Spirit. Perfection may be attained through *karma yoga* only if one dedicates all the fruits of his actions to God. This is a very important point to remember.

We Are Completely Dependent on God

As a temporal, mortal being, why should man think he has an automatic right to the things of this world? He doesn't even know why he came on earth, nor when he will leave it. We are all completely dependent upon God, who brought us here. We are on this earth to perform our God-given duties to the best of our ability, and to lay the results at His feet. We are sustained by God during every moment of our existence; not only now, but throughout all eternity. How sad when man forsakes the very One who gives him life!

"Give everything to God," Guruji said, "even the responsibility for your actions. He wants you to make Him responsible, for He is the true Doer of everything through you. You have attempted to rob Him of both the fruits of your actions and the responsibility for performing them." Morning, noon, and night the ordinary man is engrossed in "I, me, and mine." By contrast how impressive, how inspiring, our Guru's sweet humility! When anyone praised him, an ineffably tender smile would steal over his face, and he would say, "It is He who is the Doer, not I."

Paramahansaji taught, "When this 'I' shall die,

then will I know who am I." When ego consciousness is gone, one can truly live in this realization: "Lord, if any good I do in this world, it is because of You. For the mistakes I make, please forgive me, and help me to do better next time."

Never Harbor a Fear of God

God does not vindictively punish man for human mistakes. He is a very kind, forgiving, and loving Lord. Never harbor a fear of Him. Even as a child I resisted the philosophical concept of a vengeful God. I could not accept a God who sternly chastised His children for their errors, their sins. Does one love that kind of father? The child lives in fear of and runs away from a parent who wrathfully strikes or spanks him when he does wrong. We are like children before the Divine. He knows human weakness and man's susceptibility to *maya,* His cosmic delusion. Even before we commit a wrong action, He knows it. When we err, we ought to recognize our mistake and go to Him, childlike, to seek forgiveness and to ask for His blessing that tomorrow we may do better. To get in the habit of communicating with God in this way deepens one's relationship with Him. In that closeness, based upon love and the sincere effort of the devotee to do better, God is not going to punish His child.

Remind God of His Responsible Part in Our Difficulties

The Lord created this great delusion in which man is wallowing. Remind Him that it is His fault. If He had not created the cosmic delusion of *maya,* man would not be influenced to behave wrongly. After having alluded to His responsible part in our difficulties, we ought then to ask the Divine One to give us strength to tear aside the veil of delusion, so that we might always see what is Truth. We should care not what the rest of the world does, or even whether it accepts or rejects us; we should want only and always to see, and to live by, Truth.

One may not be popular with the world, but to attain worldly recognition is not why man is here. He is supposed to strive to find favor with God, to be accepted by God. It is the Lord's standards, not man's, by which we should live. See what has happened to God's creation because man lives by worldly standards! Society is in such a condition that we don't trust our statesmen, our politicians, our teachers, our parents, our young people—no one trusts anyone else. What a tragic state! How are we going to correct it? We must begin by trusting God. Faith in our Creator, and constant remembrance of the very Source of life, is what is missing.

Man must reclaim his lost divine heritage. Like the prodigal son in Jesus' parable, man is a runaway child who ought to make the effort to go back to the Divine Father. One need not don the ocher robe of the renunciant. True simplicity and freedom lie in the heart. There God silently watches you, silently guides you. There, in the feeling of love and surrender, one must establish the habit of talking with Him.

The striving devotee ought also to adopt a neutral attitude toward life; not callous indifference, but rather, as Paramahansaji has said, "Instead of cultivating endless desires, which do not always bring happiness, think of life in this way: 'Lord, you have put me in this body. I didn't ask to be born. It is You who are dreaming my existence.'" In other words, realize that you, and all other forms of life, are but condensed or materialized thoughts of God. All that we are, all that we have, belongs to Him; of ourselves we are nothing. In Him, we have everything; in Him, we are everything. In that consciousness let us perform good works, let us enjoy the good fruits of this life.

Secrets of Spiritual Progress

Self-Realization Fellowship Ashram Center, Encinitas, California, May 25, 1967

To form spiritual habits it is essential to have a set of spiritual guideposts. Paramahansa Yogananda said he disliked rules, but that in the beginning they are necessary to the seeking devotee. When one has learned how to behave, rules are unnecessary.

Interpreted in the light of Swami Sri Yukteswarji's wisdom, "how to behave" means right attitude and action born of unbroken attunement with God. When we find ourselves always in His consciousness, we no longer need rules. Until then we do need their discipline. We should not think of spiritual rules as confining. They are friends, helping to guide us, to channel our energies, thoughts, and activities in a constructive way that leads Godward.

We can best understand rules and willingly follow them when we realize that correct behavior can be summed up in this way: *doing the things we ought to do when we ought to do them.* The individual who has acquired this art of right behavior needs no rules; yet he continues to follow the same principles as before, without any sense of restriction. For example, we have in our ashrams the rule of daily group meditation. When a person attains the understanding and ability to "do the things he ought to do when he ought to do them," this rule is no longer a rule for him. He automatically follows it because the habit of right behavior is set, and because he finds in this practice the way of life that he wants to establish. He *wants* to be with God.

If water is allowed to flow indiscriminately over the land, it acts as a destructive force. In order to utilize water power for some constructive purpose, man must first build a dam to control the water's flow and direction. Its power is then constructively harnessed. It is the same with spiritual effort. If we channel it, it is productive. Wise rules do not hinder, but rather take us in a desired direction in a straightforward, regulated way. On the spiritual path they are an essential part of life.

Students of Self-Realization Fellowship should make the principles taught by Paramahansa Yogananda their "rules" or guideposts, following the spiritual routine he prescribed; they will see how effectively their efforts are guided Godward. At the head of the list will be the rule of daily meditation balanced by right activity.

The Conflict Between Service and Meditation

This question often arises in the mind of one who is deeply seeking God: "What is the relationship between service and meditation? Where does my duty lie — in constructive activity or in meditation?" Ultimately, the highest form of action is meditation; therefore it should not be neglected, even if the devotee's other duties suffer a little as a result.

God is both active and inactive. Without His activity there could be no creation. At the same time, as the Absolute beyond all creation, He is eternally still. If we are the soul made in His image—not one whit less than

Himself—then our nature, too, is both active and inactive. The goal of every person who would know God is to learn how to combine these two qualities in his life.

It is ideal if such an individual has the drive, will power, determination, and devotion to sit for eight, ten, twelve hours a day in deep meditation. I don't mean just sitting there absentmindedly, sometimes falling asleep and then "coming to" again, but meditating deeply. But unless the aspirant has already attained a high degree of spiritual progress, he will not be able to maintain the meditative state for such prolonged periods. For the average man on the spiritual path, therefore, work, performed as a service to God, is also essential. One's whole desire should lean toward meditation; there is no question about it. But one should also combine with this desire the spirit of selfless activity.

The Bhagavad Gita tells us that we must learn to be active, not for self, but for God; and that we must combine action with meditation. This is the substance of the philosophy preached to Arjuna by Lord Krishna in the Gita. Like almost everyone else in this active world, I have never had the opportunity to be wholly free from activity. But I made up my mind at the beginning that every free moment was going to be filled with God. That is the essential: to be fully active for God, doing everything for Him, and to use one's free moments to think only of Him. This is the way to balance and combine in one's life these two principles of action and inaction.

A perceptive student once asked me: "Is it not a form of temptation when one is inspired to leave his meditation, or to shorten his meditation, or to miss his meditation in order to perform some kind of service?"

Yes, it is. We have certain duties—we cannot discount that—but there are many times when we occupy ourselves with tasks that could well be done later, after we have fulfilled our need for meditation. In addition, whenever we have finished our duties, the moment we think of meditation we should lay aside any other diversion and meditate. The evening hours and afterhours should be occupied with this kind of effort to know God.

Meditation Is Our Most Important Duty

After taking care of his other responsibilities, one should get into the habit of retiring into seclusion to meditate deeply. This habit we were taught to cultivate very early on the path. The following practice I found most helpful: One day a week I would quit my ashram duties at five, forgo my evening meal, and retire to my room and begin meditation. I would not leave my meditation seat until midnight. The spiritual strength, the divine blessing that this practice gave me, no words can describe. Everyone who will devoutly follow this principle of making a real effort to make time for God will find his progress greatly hastened.

Meditation is our most important duty. It establishes a relationship with God that in turn gives meaning to everything else in life. Therefore we should first meditate, then perform our other duties. Much of the time when we neglect meditation we invent excuses to justify our not meditating. Too often we prefer to rationalize. "Why should I not let my duties go and just meditate?" or "I have too many duties, so I have no time to meditate." Thus we reason when we want an excuse for not working or for not meditating. If one truly desires God, he won't let anything stand in his way. He may have duties; he must perform them. But he will not accept the idea that duties are a limitation on his search for God. This is the right attitude.

Seeking and finding God takes tremendous will power and self-discipline. We do not gain the Highest Treasure simply by a few halfhearted prayers or by a few good works. We gain that Treasure by self-discipline, by will power applied to meditation and to right action, right performance of one's duties.

Man could not reason, he could not even lift a finger, unless God gave him the power to do so. Therefore it is God who is the Doer. We are merely His instruments. When one maintains this realization while performing his duties, his actions become a form of meditation. As one thinks, so he becomes. Meditation, a state of inner attunement with God, is a condition that can be applied to every activity and function of our lives.

A Change in Our Thinking Will Bring God Nearer

Because God is, we are. He is the only principle in life; there is nothing outside Him. It follows logically that we must be a part of Him. The feeling of separateness from God is a delusion. We can help break this delusion by changing our thinking. No matter what we are doing, the mind is always thinking something. So let your mind think about God and inwardly talk to Him.

While outwardly caring for the body, for example, be thinking within: "This body is God's temple. I have nothing to do with it, except to take care of it for Him to use in whatever way He will. How He will use it or whether or not He will sustain it is His affair, not mine. I will take healthful care of this body, not because I am interested in it or because it is something I am bound by, or want to hold on to, but because I am maintaining it for Him."

In striving to keep our minds on God while performing our duties, we shouldn't be absentminded, of course; but every now and then the mind should be saying, "Lord, if it were not for Your strength and intelligence pouring through this vehicle, I could do nothing." When one develops inner communion with God in deep meditation, his mind can be immersed in God, he can be mentally conversing with Him, no matter what he is doing. This is expressed by Paramahansa Yogananda in his beautiful poem, *God! God! God!* "In waking, eating, working, dreaming, sleeping, serving, meditating, chanting, divinely loving [all my loved ones], my soul constantly hums, unheard by any: 'God! God! God!'" Paramahansaji lived his whole life that way. It is possible to do so. When there is constant remembrance of God, one day He suddenly responds. Then what joy floods the whole being! That joy sustains the devotee on the spiritual path.

Perform Duties Willingly, Without Complaint

In performance of our duties we should never complain. We should be on fire with enthusiasm every moment, no matter what tasks fall to our lot. When we whine, when we are negative, we shut off God's power and our contact with Him. While doing our best, we should keep always positive and cheerful and feel a sense of surrender to God. This gives a peace, a tranquillity, that nothing else in this world can give.

And we must also be willing. We have to watch our motives so that we don't try to deceive ourselves when we avoid a duty. Even though we can give the most logical of reasons for saying "No," we know when we are really saying it because we don't want to do that particular task; we know when we are saying "No" because we secretly have a negative attitude.

One should work enthusiastically and creatively to fulfill his duties and serve God, yet not be afflicted with pride of accomplishment. Certainly we are happy when we do something well. Everyone wants to feel some satisfaction from what he has done. There is nothing wrong with that. But we must avoid the egoistic thought, "*I* did it." That is where pride steps in. When someone speaks words of praise about us we should immediately acknowledge God inwardly: "Lord, I know You are the Doer. By myself, I know nothing. Of myself, I can do nothing. If I am able to accomplish anything worthwhile in this life, it is only because of the intelligence and faith with which You have endowed me." This practice refers the credit to God, where it belongs. One cannot then feel egoistic pride.

As Souls All Men Are Equal

There is another way to avoid pride: Realize that we are all equal before God; in His eyes none are greater or lesser. When death comes, one is severed from all his material accomplishments. Wherein, then, is their importance? The Lord is not interested in whether one is a great scientist, or a great orator, or a great writer, or whether one has attained stature according to the standards of the world. Such achievements do not afford us any significant spiritual knowledge. Realization of the soul is the only attainment that has lasting value, that will not be taken away by death. Spiritual principles are a great leveler of man's ego!

One of the qualities I so deeply respected in our guru, Paramahansa Yogananda, was that he treated everyone as a soul. He did not place some higher or lower according to their abilities or status in life. He could not be bribed by anyone's power or position. His one standard was: "Do you love God and want to find Him?" That is all that mattered to him. Jesus set this example. His disciples were not men of great worldly learning and accomplishments. Those twelve apostles, who were given the responsibility of spreading a message that has already lasted two thousand years, came from the humblest walks of life; some were mere fishermen. This shows that it is not what man has achieved in the world that counts, but what man achieves in his struggle to know God, in his effort to be in tune with God.

Last but not least, one should do everything with all his intelligence and ability; but having done it, he should not be attached to the results of his works. This is what the Gita teaches. When one can learn to perform all duties with great enthusiasm, yet retain a nonattached attitude toward the results, he will find tremendous mental freedom.

The Only Good Is God

The person who seeks God earnestly comes to realize that everything he ever wanted, from human relationships or from the world, he receives from the One. From God comes all the praise and encouragement that his soul yearns for. From God he receives all the love that his soul has craved throughout incarnations. From God he receives all the wisdom, understanding, and happiness that he has sought from others and from things of this world. From the one Absolute he receives strength to stand alone, unshaken by any blows of circumstance. This is the kind of strength and self-containment each one of us wants, because our soul knows that it is independent and all-powerful, being made in the image of God, and hence endowed with His qualities. Man's suffering is due to his soul's torment that it cannot demonstrate its all-powerful nature. The limitations man has placed on himself are hidden cords with which he has bound his soul.

Meditation frees the soul from those bonds; and right activity is an expression of the soul's freedom and all-perfect, all-joyous nature.

Is Meditation on God Compatible with Modern Life?

Condensation of a talk at
Self-Realization Fellowship international headquarters,
Los Angeles, California, February 12, 1970

The ultimate goal is that which you experience in meditation—not the spoken word; not the written word. The truths that Paramahansa Yogananda and all of the great ones have taught down through the ages are not the end in themselves. They merely serve as a golden rule, the divine standards or laws by which we can directly experience a blissful, loving, intoxicating relationship with God. Never let the spoken or the written word stand in the way of that deep realization. This means that one should not become lost in the words, but in the *experience,* the realization, of the truths they describe. So many people become engrossed in an intellectual understanding of truth, and forget the ultimate goal.

Someone has asked this question: "I meditate again and again and reach a certain borderline that I am not able to go beyond. Sometimes it seems that my consciousness starts to expand, but as soon as I turn to my daily duties that connection with God is snapped apart. The experiences in meditation have not yet become a part of my daily experience. I have not yet found an answer to my question, whether the busy life of a

Westerner is compatible with meditation. A feeling tells me that the Absolute can be grasped only in deepest silence and peace. But how can that be accomplished when one also must serve his fellowmen in this busy life?"

Combine Meditation with Right Activity

If we go to the Bhagavad Gita, and the words of Jesus in the Bible, we are taught that the true path to Self-realization is the path that combines meditation with right activity. Both are essential in order to experience divine consciousness.

When I first came to the ashram many years ago, I had one dream, and that was to devote myself, as many hours a day as I could, to long and deep meditation. There was no thought in my mind to do organizational work. I served in the kitchen, in the gardens, in the office, as well as fulfilling my duties as secretary to Guruji; I did everything that was asked of me, but there was no desire other than to get to God, to have His divine contact as fast as I could. But I noticed that as often as I tried to remain only on the meditative level of activity, Master pulled me back into the work. For a long time this troubled me, until one day he said to me: "You must realize this: seeking God means also to serve Him in mankind. You cannot be wholly immersed in God's divine consciousness until you have learned how to balance your life with meditation plus right activity."

Guruji meant that truth not only for those of us who live in ashrams, but for the whole world. It is absolutely essential in order to be a balanced individual. When I think of "balance," I always relate it to the one human being I have met in my life who in my opinion was absolutely, perfectly balanced—and that was Master. Wholly immersed in God, he was also wholly engrossed in selfless dedication to God's work. That is my ideal. Now, how to get to that state? The pattern has been laid before you. Master often said, referring to the devout followers of all religious paths, "Just as the Christian Scientist, before he begins his day, studies the lesson for the day from his *Science and Health,* which is his holy scripture; and just as the Catholic goes every morning to attend Mass; so the faithful follower of Self-Realization sets aside a solitude-period morning and evening to devote himself to deep meditation."

Meditation Alone Can Satisfy Your Spiritual Hunger

Unless and until you have formed the habit of daily meditation, morning and night, you will not be able to satisfy your own soul; and you will not be pleasing God. This applies to all of our members around the world. In the life of a Self-Realizationist there is a time every morning and every night that should be as important as, and even more important than, the time set aside for eating and sleeping. When a devotee will have that conviction and that yearning and that determination to make a time every day for God, just as he makes a time for food and sleep, then—you may know for certain—he is going to reach his goal. But unfortunately, so many, many other habits have been formed, not only during this life but in many past lives, that we try to flee from this responsibility, from this divine duty. But there is no valid reason for which you can ever say that you have not had the opportunity to seek God deeply in meditation. You are fooling yourself, but you are not fooling God.

"To thine own self be true; and it must follow, as the night the day, thou canst not then be false to any man."* Most people do not understand the meaning of those words. "To thine own self be true" does not mean, be true to the little ego-consciousness, the little *id* that resides within; but to the God within you be true. That is a vital point on the spiritual path.

This idea that Master brought to the West, that man should seek God and also devote himself to his duties—how are you to do it? First of all, set your mind upon what you want to achieve in life; you have to be honest here. You may think there are lots of things you want: "I want money. I want name. I want position. I want all of these things." But if you honestly use your discrimination, and if you can learn from the mistakes of others, you can look around and see all of the people who have achieved the very things that you want, but still have not found the goal of life, which is happiness.

"But seek ye first the kingdom of God...and all these things shall be added unto you."† Are these false words that merely soothe mankind into a state of spiritual apathy?‡ Or do they carry the living spirit of God, the living wisdom of God? For myself, I can say beyond any question: I know the truth of that great statement. Seek ye God first, then all the things you

* Hamlet, Act I, Scene 3.

† Matthew 6:33.

‡ That is, the mistaken supposition that we have only to sit and pray and God will give us everything we need. Without real spiritual effort to conquer our imperfections; without sincere endeavor to dive deep in meditation; without physical effort to look after ourselves and to fulfill our responsibilities and be of service to God in this world, the divine law of fulfillment will not work for us.

have ever craved will be added unto you. I find there is nothing I want. Complete contentment is within me.

In my meditation just now, as I experienced that great bliss and intoxicating love of God, I thought: "O God, if only the world knew what one can experience within this heart, this vast temple within!"—a complete sense of fulfillment, which has nothing to do with the flesh, but which so consumes the soul that night and day you want only to remain in that state of consciousness.

Be Sincere in Your Spiritual Goals

So first, know what your goal is, and set for yourself those steps, or guideposts, by which you can go toward that goal. First and foremost, meditate! Even when you don't feel like it, meditate. Even when your body is unwell, get in the habit of meditating anyway. Even when you're tired, don't let your body lie on that bed first. You have to have that kind of determination. If you learn this principle, it becomes a spiritual backbone to you. The man who finds God is the man who has a backbone: not only a moral backbone, but a sound emotional backbone, and above all, a spiritual backbone. These three are necessary.

So, know what your goal is and never compromise it, even when you're tempted to do so. Those individuals who give up because of some discontentment in life or in their relationship with other people, I see how fast they go downhill, getting farther and farther away from the very center or hub of the wheel of the spiritual life. Master often used to say to us, "If you want to know God, don't remain on the rim." As in the game children play at a carnival or on a playground, if you get very close to the center of a revolving wheel, no matter how fast it goes, you can't be thrown off; but if you stay on the rim, the first thing you know you are thrown off. It is the same with the spiritual path.

And next must be this [Daya Mata reads question submitted to her]: "I have heard it said that there are teachers who claim that it is not necessary to discipline oneself." To that statement I say, "Utter, *utter* nonsense." This cannot be! You cannot know God unless you have learned how to master yourself. It is impossible. The man whose mind is filled with jealousy; the man whose mind is filled with envy; the man whose mind is filled with sensual thoughts shuts God out. You cannot have light and dark in the same place at the same time. You cannot have simultaneously in your mind the consciousness of God and these very human thoughts. It is impossible. How are you going to remove those wrong thoughts except by self-discipline? There is no other way. I think the problem is that many people do not understand what discipline means.

Positive, Right Thinking

If you want to drive darkness out of a room, you don't use a flyswatter and keep hitting at the darkness, do you? Because even if you could do that a thousand years, you would not drive it away. The way to drive darkness out of the room is to turn on the light, or strike a match. The way to overcome your negative thinking is to apply its opposite, positive thinking. The moment you begin to think in a more positive way in your life, the more you begin to speak in a more positive way, the more you begin to act in a more positive way, know for certain you are applying those divine laws that will automatically draw to you the good result of those laws.

So along with daily meditation, it is essential that an individual learn to watch his thoughts, because thought is the father or the parent of the deed. "For as he thinketh in his heart, so is he."* What you think, you eventually express in your words and in your deeds. So one has to begin in himself, with his thoughts. One has to begin to replace negative, critical, doubting thoughts with positive thoughts; and the simplest way to do this, in my own experience, is this: As often as you have time free from your duties, let your mind rest in God. He is the most powerful thought in the world. This is called practicing the presence of God. The mind is like a blank road when you are born. Your thoughts then begin to cut grooves in your brain. When you take a particular thought—especially if it's a negative or destructive one—and again and again and again think it, and no one ever trains or disciplines you to get out of that groove, you will find as you get older the time comes when you absolutely are bound by that thought, and you cannot free yourself.

Think of God Day and Night

So it is important on the spiritual path, if you want to know God, to begin to cut new grooves in your brain, new grooves of positive, devotional thoughts about God. Whether you are a teacher, or working with mathematics, or lecturing, or cooking in a kitchen as a housewife, or doing any other kind of work, every moment cut one single groove: "My God, my God, my God, my God." You mustn't be absentminded though. All the time I am thinking: "O my Lord, show me the

* Proverbs 23:7.

way to please You. I want to live in this world only to please You." I find such intoxicating joy in that. I can't imagine any other way of living. It is blissful. Every time you take His name you find a fresh flow of joy, a fresh flow of love pouring into your heart, pouring into your consciousness.

Practice the presence of God, and meditate; this is the way one learns how to live happily amongst his fellowmen in this world. You don't have to tell everybody your feelings. In fact, it is a great mistake to tell others about your spiritual life. The moment you do it, you lose something of your spiritual strength. Guruji told us that. You may have found it so in your own case; you had a wonderful experience, but the moment you told it to someone you suddenly felt, "Oh! I have lost something." There was an intrusion of another person's consciousness upon something that was so sacred to you. This is why Guruji always told us devotees, "Don't talk about your divine experiences." It's different if we're in *satsanga* like this, and if it helps you all. But don't feel the need to talk of your experiences to other people. The greatest way we can influence them is by spiritualizing our life, our deeds, our thoughts.

To come back to the question: Is it possible that the busy life of a Westerner is compatible with meditation? It is completely possible. It is perfectly logical. It is what God intended of man when He created us. We are to perform all our duties in this world with enthusiasm, with great joy, with deep attention to whatever we are doing, but always with the thought, "I am doing it for You, my God."

That kind of enthusiasm must be in all of us on the spiritual path. There is nothing worse than the individual who is just halfhearted about his spiritual life. That is a tragedy, to me. And it's just as much a tragedy to see the person who goes through life, as Master used to say, as if he had no life in him at all; you shake his hand and it's like clasping a dead fish.

Do your work in this world, but follow the ideal of the *karma* yogi:* "I diligently perform all my duties, my Lord, but not for myself. I don't care whether You put me here, or down here [Mataji gestures, to illustrate]. What I care about is that You are with me wherever You put me. I shall work dutifully, with no thought of pleasing anyone but You; with no thought of any credit for myself, with no thought of praise from anyone. My Lord, if I can please You, that is everything to me." It would be ideal if mankind learned how to apply this principle. Then we would find a world filled with peace and contentment and happiness. That is what has to come in this civilization if we are ever to have peace.

Meaning of Responsibility

We have to begin to enjoy working. The man who goes out and sleeps in the park, and who has no responsibilities and doesn't care about anyone else, that's not the ideal. We have gone from one extreme to another. We have to learn to be responsible human beings. This is what God expects of us.

"Responsible" means that we express that which we are—all of those qualities that have to do with the soul. And when we begin to do this, then we are living in this world as God intended man to live. We perform all our actions with our minds fixed upon Him.

* One who follows the path of *Karma Yoga*. (See page 116.)

As in the story of Sukadeva and King Janaka, learn to keep your attention constantly upon the oil of God-awareness while performing all your duties in this world.* Move through life fulfilling—not shirking!—all duties that God sends to you each day. Use them as an offering to Him: "My Lord, I cannot give You gold. I cannot give You wisdom. There is nothing I can give You, for You already have everything. What can I give You, my Lord? I can give You my humble service every day of my life. Wherever I can sow the seeds of goodwill, wherever I can be a peacemaker, wherever I can speak constructively, wherever I can do any good, there I am not serving myself—I am serving You."

Constructive and Destructive Sensitivity

One of the greatest arts to be learned in this life is how to get along easily with people, without much conflict. I think of my own first meetings with Master. He had that remarkable capacity to make anyone who came to him feel perfectly at home—it was as if he had known you always. You felt as if you could open your heart wide to him from the first moment. He had that ability to project from himself the essence of what he was: an embodiment of the divine qualities of friendship and love and goodwill.

We should learn to so behave in this world that we

* To test the young Sukadeva before accepting him as a disciple, the great saint King Janaka required Sukadeva to tour the palace while carrying in the palm of his hand an oil lamp filled to the brim. The condition of passing the test was that Sukadeva was to observe minutely (and subsequently report to the King) every item and detail in each palatial room, without spilling one drop of oil from the brimful lamp.

don't offend others needlessly. You know how some people always go around with a chip on their shoulder. It seems as if you devote your whole life to thinking, "Now, how can I avoid disturbing that chip on his shoulder? I have to be careful how I say things, so that I don't offend him." We all go through this. I'll tell you how Master dealt with it! Any time he saw someone with a chip on his shoulder, he used to say, "You must overcome your sensitivity." Don't be so self-centered. The person with a chip on his shoulder—analyze it—is the individual who is so much wrapped up in himself that he's constantly on guard, trying to protect himself from what he thinks are the gibes of other people. This is wrong. We have to learn how to grow a little tougher hide. Guruji said that to me years ago. I was extremely sensitive, I suffered a great deal from it long before I met Master. I never wanted to hurt others, and I kept away from people lest I be hurt by them. During the War* I suffered a great deal. I thought of all the boys being maimed or killed, and it really gave me much sorrow.

Master said to me one day, "You know, if you expect to get through life, you must learn how to be tough."

I replied, "Master, I don't like hard people."

"Don't misunderstand me," he said. "I do not mean that kind of hardness wherein one has no sympathy for others. But unless and until you have developed within you a certain spiritual strength, a spiritual fiber, you cannot help others, and you cannot help yourself."

* World War II.

The moment someone becomes negative and weak, in your great sympathy you plunge into the same hole of delusion with him. You can't lift him out, then. The divine man, even though he suffers within, even though he has his own crosses, doesn't let anyone else know. He silently bears his burden. But if he hears of someone else's suffering, he will not go down into the pit with the individual, but will reach down to pull that person up.

In this world we can't help sometimes hurting others. It isn't possible to go through life without hurting some people some of the time. Even Christ couldn't do it. Even Master couldn't do it. We must realize that because people are made the way they are, we are bound sometimes to rub some of them the wrong way. On the other hand, understanding that point, we ought not to be so touchy, so sensitive, if someone rubs *us* the wrong way. Always try to put yourself in the other individual's shoes. Try to understand a thing from his viewpoint, and try never to take anything too personally. It is impossible to deal with an individual if he constantly involves himself personally in the discussion. It is better, when you are discussing things, to keep to principles. Avoid personalities. Then you can avoid much misunderstanding.

I am bringing out these points for one reason: We are asking, "How can we bring God into our daily lives?" The answer is, by this kind of self-discipline. It is not enough merely to repeat a *mantram** and say that

* *Mantram* or *mantra,* in the general sense, is the science of root sounds which by sympathetic vibration have a correspondence with creation itself. In the spiritual sense, certain sounds are chanted vocally or mentally to help calm and spiritualize the mind.

we can thereby do away with all self-discipline and still know God. You cannot do it. You have to back up your *mantrams* and your practice of God's presence by right thinking and by right actions; for it is meditation *and* right activity, as the Gita teaches, that give man God-realization.

You cannot go around talking God all day long, and at the same time ride roughshod over other people, and still have God-communion. It is impossible. If relationships with others were not necessary to our growth, God would have put each man in his own little world where he could do nothing but think of God all day. But He knew that was not the way for us to attain oneness with Him again. He took millions of us, a conglomeration of millions of different kinds of personalities and characteristics and tendencies, and threw us onto this earth, you might say, into all kinds of environments; and then He said to us, "Now, learn how to get along with each other!" And that applies not only to devotees living in ashrams, but to the whole world.

Right activity involves learning how to get along with your fellowman. Right activity cannot come about without self-discipline. It is the very basis of the spiritual life.

Man is made in the image of God; and unless and until he learns how to free that divine image from the cage of this fleshly form, and from the invisible cage of his moods and habits and emotions, he cannot know God. The only way he can free himself from these visible and invisible cages in which the soul has found itself caught is by discipline of the self. Self-mastery is the true meaning of the word *swami*. He who would know God must learn to master himself. He must learn to free the caged soul from the bonds of flesh, from the bonds of his emotions, from the bonds of his habits; then he will know what he is. Then he will know he is made in the image of God. He can move through this world as a free soul, performing all of his duties with greater enthusiasm than the ordinary man who performs his duties in order to acquire gold or fame. The divine man is willing and ready to give totally of himself in his service to God—plus meditation. The two are necessary.

Meditation and Right Thinking

Meditation is the ability to take the mind away from every object of distraction and put it upon God alone. There are many different kinds of meditation. There is meditation as practiced by the Christian mystic. There is meditation as practiced by the Hindu mystic, the yogi. There is meditation as practiced in the other great religions of the world. All paths lead to God. This is what we teach, and what we believe. Without some form of meditation, God cannot be known. Meditation alone, however, is not enough. Along with meditation one must begin to guide his thoughts. When he is tempted to think evil thoughts about others, when he has a desire to strike back at someone who has hit him, when he has a desire to hurt someone by his words, at that moment he disciplines himself: "I will not do it!" For a very simple reason he won't do it; he finds that the moment he allows mean thoughts to enter his consciousness, in that instant the divine light goes out, and darkness descends upon him. I have often thought of this in my own life. Many times through the early years there were occasions when Daya Ma was hurt. This is what I used to say to Divine Mother: "You see, I am very selfish. I am not going to allow any dark thoughts, or thoughts of resentment or hatred to enter this heart, because I have found that the moment these come in, You fly; and I'm not going to let You go. So Divine Mother, it is for You to fight my battles for me if I need defending in this world. It is for me to think of You. You worry about me if You want to; I am concerned only with You."

That kind of philosophy brings a sweet relationship with God. It establishes such an intimate, devotional feeling for God. It makes you realize He is really nearest of the near. Whom else will I go to, to talk over all my difficulties, but God? Who else has the wisdom to guide aright, but my God? He is also the dearest of the dear. Who else loves me without any condition, but God? Who else will understand me even when I fail to understand myself, but my God? Who is closer to me than my God? because even those whom I cherish and love so much, one day I must leave. But I find there is an unbroken continuity of my awareness of that Beloved One; and I shall cling to that awareness, that thought of my Beloved, through all the changes this life shall go through. When you begin to think in these terms, you find such sweet rapport with God. You find that He is always with you; there is no separation. When that state comes, you do not ever want to lose it for any reason. You find that you are aflame to spread His divine message throughout the world.

Your Real Mission in Life

I don't know how the world lives without thinking of God! You have heard the expression, "marooned in space." That's a modern term of this day and age, isn't it! The world is marooned in its delusions. This is a tragedy; unfortunately, we begin to make an effort to save ourselves only when some sorrow comes into our lives. I don't believe we should wait for that. We should at this moment resolve that God put us here for a reason. "Why was I born?" The moment we begin to ask that question, so many of us in delusion become convinced we were born to be great messiahs—and that's another delusion! The one mission in the world that all of us were put here to perform is to save ourselves! First save yourself, and then maybe God will use you as an instrument to try to save others. Isn't that being honest with yourself? So many want to save the world before they have even begun to save themselves. I am saying this because sometimes devotees write letters and say, "I know God has a great mission for me." And I want to say to them, "Yes, that great mission is to save *you!*"

Devote yourself *now* to deep, long meditation. Devote yourself *now* to overcoming the little self, that the greater Self might become more manifest within you. That was the training Master gave us all.

And so, my dear ones, I have given you these suggestions: Daily meditate, and daily watch your thoughts. Discipline your mind when you find yourself becoming filled with dark thoughts. God has given you discrimination, the ability to discern the difference between right and wrong. When you find yourself going in the wrong direction, stop at that moment. Turn around, and begin to think of God. "God, give me strength. Help me to overcome this."

If you have a violent temper, discipline yourself. Master used to say to us, "Bite your tongue before you speak a harsh word." And I used to practice it. Then I saw one day: "Look here, every time you lose your temper, what is happening? You also lose your peace. Who is suffering? Whom are you punishing? Only yourself. This is ridiculous." If you have a bad temper and want to pick up things and throw them on the floor, get out and take a walk. Walk, walk, walk, but don't think about the thing you have left behind. Try to think of the beauties of nature, or try to divert your mind into some other constructive avenue. And if you feel hatred, remember: what you send out, the Divine Law brings back to you; he who hates will be hated in this world. The moment you begin to hate somebody, in the next instant think to yourself, "This is a boomerang that will come back to me! Lord, bless that soul! Lord, bless that soul!" As often as the hatred wells up in you: "Bless that soul, Lord, bless that soul." The more you think this, the more you will really want God to bless that soul. This actually happens.

You can take this principle and apply it to all of the different struggles you face. This is the practical way to apply the teachings of Self-Realization. This is practicing the presence of God also, applying His divine principles in your daily life.

[Sri Daya Mata leads the group in prayer and meditation, concluding the *satsanga* with the following remarks.]

Do not spill the peace and the understanding that you receive during meditation, when you leave meditation. Carry with you as long as you can, throughout the day, the thought of God and the peace that you gather in the pail of your consciousness during meditation. This is the way that one learns to hold on to God in the midst of all one's activities. In the words of Master, "We must learn to be calmly active, actively calm; a prince of peace sitting on the throne of poise, directing our kingdom of activity."

The Only Way to Happiness

New Delhi, India, December 3, 1961

We must realize that we are the perfect, immortal soul. The imperfections we express through our habits and moods, through sickness and failure, are not a part of our real nature. We have so deeply identified ourselves with mortal consciousness that we unthinkingly accept its limitations. Rather, we should pray, "Lord, help me to realize that I am not this body, not my moods and habits. Make me know that I am ever Thy child, made in Thy flawless image."

One day during meditation I was bemoaning the fact that there was so much imperfection in me, when suddenly I heard the sweet voice of the Mother saying, "But do you love Me?" At once my whole being was bursting with the love for Her that flooded me. From that day to this my mind has been absorbed in one thought: "I am in love with my Divine Mother, and in that love my life is surrendered to Her, to do with as She wishes." I have complete faith in Her; I know that Her love will never fail me.

God loves all of you in the same way. The sunlight shines equally on the charcoal and the diamond. One cannot say that the sun is partial because the diamond reflects more light than the charcoal. Similarly, the sunlight of God's love shines equally on all. We must become like the diamond, which receives and reflects His light.

Unceasingly take the name of the Divine, not with absentmindedness, but with full attention. God-communion requires our utmost concentration. No matter what we are doing outwardly, our deeper mind can be absorbed in the One alone, ever whispering, "Thou art my only love."

The Most Successful Man

It is God's love that comes to us through all human forms. If you seek Him first, then everything else you have ever craved will come to you. I have found beyond doubt that everything man hungers for is to be found in the Cosmic Beloved. Great devotees of God have been the inspiration of humanity since time began. Who has been the most successful man—complete within himself; understanding himself and the rest of the world; remembered and honored through the ages by the world—who has been that kind of man? He who has known God.

Our blessed guru, Paramahansa Yogananda, said that to be that kind of successful human being we must first of all have a desire for God. Usually man does not have that desire until some adversity comes. When life is flowing smoothly, man feels no need for the Lord. But when his whole way of life seems suddenly swept away—if he loses his health, wealth, or a loved one—then he begins to cry to God for help.

Gurudeva urged us to seek God first, for only with our consciousness anchored in Him can we win the battle of life. When we are brought face to face with difficult times by this ever-changing world, we must be divine warriors. Why wait for life to take us by surprise, to disillusion us, to beat us down? Let us cultivate the desire for God *now* and begin our search for Him. He who is with us in times of peace will not forsake us in the hours of trial.

Steps Toward Self-Realization

The first step toward Self-realization is yearning, divine yearning for God. By daily meditation we develop the habit of loving Him. Every human being should spend a little time each day in deep communion with God. Man is eager to keep his body well and comfortable, and sometimes he makes an effort to develop his intelligence, but what time out of the twenty-four hours a day does he devote to his soul, his real self? Hardly any. Even when he does his *japa** or *puja*† or says his prayers, his mind is scattered and restless. We must be sincere with God. What is the use of saying, "Lord, I love You," if the mind is away on something else? But take the name of God and say it just once with pure love, or over and over chant it with ever deeper yearning and concentration, and it will change your life.

Devotees like me will come again and again to speak to you about God, and you may read countless books about Him, but neither of these will give you divine attainment. By your own effort you must dig Him out of His invisible omnipresence. You have only to take your mind within, away from the consciousness of the body, and you will find that One.

The purpose of life is to know God. We must know

* Repetition of a *mantra* or a name of God.

† Ceremonial worship.

Him, because the primordial disease of mankind is ignorance, and only by communion with the all-knowing Power shall we be able to free ourselves from the effects of this ignorance.

In addition to cultivating yearning for God, the devotee should strive for simplicity. Keep life simple and uncomplicated. Don't desire unnecessary things. The West has too much luxury; India has too much poverty. Gurudeva used to say that there should be a balance between the spiritual ideals of the East and the material efficiency of the West. Too much, as well as too little, ultimately brings misery. "High thinking and simple living" is the best formula for a happy life. Keep your thoughts lofty, for the power of the mind is great.

Next comes right action: to do what we ought to do when we ought to do it. Most of the time our actions are under the compulsive direction of our habits. Right action is governed not by habit, but by the principle of truth. In India right action is summed up by "*yama*" and "*niyama*,"* which correspond to the Ten Commandments of the Christian world. Live by these principles. Be honest with yourself. Know your true motives. This will help you to grow and to live more and more by truth.

Cheerfulness must accompany right action. When you feel sad or are in a negative mood, you can get out of that state if you make up your mind to be cheerful. Gurudeva used to say, "If you make up your mind to be happy, nothing can make you unhappy. But if you make up your mind to be unhappy, nothing can make

* The rules of moral conduct (*yama*) and religious observances (*niyama*) that form the first two steps of the "Eightfold Path of Yoga" outlined by the ancient sage Patanjali.

you happy." So make up your mind to be always cheerful. When conditions are unfavorable, keep the mind positive, remembering that the trouble is only temporary and will pass away.

Raja Yoga teaches the scientific way to commune with God. In the teaching of *Raja Yoga,* concentration means to take the attention away from all objects of distraction and to place it on one thing at a time. The principle is to still all restless thoughts so that the mind becomes like a clear, calm lake in which you can see the object of your concentration perfectly reflected. The ability to concentrate is necessary both to succeed in the world and to progress in meditation.

After attaining the state of concentration, one is ready for meditation, in which the object of concentration is God. In meditation, when the mind becomes absorbed in that One, you begin to feel an expansion of your consciousness and become filled with divine love, which overflows to all—not a possessive love, but a love that is freeing. This is God's love. It is a love that satisfies all the longings of the heart and soul. In this love is the ecstasy of God-consciousness. The soul, freed from body identification, is bathed in His blissful consciousness, and there is no desire but to remain forever in that divine ecstasy. One feels no need for anything external.

Our Kingdom Is Not of This World

Men think that this world is the only reality. But there is something beyond this world, and the reason man goes on being dissatisfied is that his kingdom is not of this world. Everything here is temporary and subject to change, governed by the illusion of time.

His Holiness, the late Jagatguru (world teacher) Sri Shankaracharya Bharati Krishna Tirth of Gowardan Math, Puri, with Sri Daya Mataji at Self-Realization Fellowship international headquarters, Los Angeles, March 1958. His Holiness was the apostolic successor of the first Shankaracharya (ninth century; India's greatest philosopher). Self-Realization Fellowship was honored to sponsor the U.S. tour of His Holiness.

On many occasions the great Jagatguru voiced his loving spiritual support of the work of Paramahansa Yogananda: "I have found in Self-Realization Fellowship the highest spirituality, service, and love. Not only do their representatives preach these principles, but they live according to them." In correspondence with Daya Mataji, he always addressed her with fatherly warmth and spiritual regard as "very dear (or beloved) child Daya Devi ('godly one')."

While engrossed in a devotional *bhajan* (worshiping God in song), Mataji's consciousness withdraws into the deep inner state of *samadhi;* Ranchi, 1967.

"O God, if only the world knew what one can experience within this heart, this vast temple within!—a complete sense of fulfillment, which has nothing to do with the flesh, but which so consumes the soul that night and day you want only to remain in that state of consciousness."

When one becomes united with the Divine, there is no past, present, or future. God alone is eternal.

Instead of talking about God, instead of reading about Him, now is the time to *feel* Him. The world will not know peace until man has learned to feel peace in God.

Man has to change himself before he can change the world. Unless and until we as individuals learn to live together as God's children, beholding the one creative Beam of light behind all forms, there will be division, war, and misery. We must find God within, and then with humility share with others His peace, love, and harmony. As we strive in this way to serve as God's instruments, we should pray, "Lord, Thou art the Doer. Thy will be done." Humbly seeking the will of God does not imply idleness or lack of initiative and action: God helps him who helps himself. It means rather to surrender to God, that He may use you as His instrument to do good on earth according to His divine will.

Set aside time every day for meditation—deep, joyous communion with God. Out of the twenty-four hours in each day give one hour to the Divine Beloved. Wise is that man who takes to heart this advice. "Life is sweet and death a dream; joy is sweet and sorrow a dream, when Thy song flows through me."* Thou art Wisdom. Thou art Bliss. Thou art Love. And That, dear ones, is your reality.

* From *Cosmic Chants,* by Paramahansa Yogananda.

Heaven Lies Within

Self-Realization Fellowship international headquarters, Los Angeles, California, September 4, 1962

The surest way to be always at peace within is to keep God in our thoughts throughout the day, no matter what we are doing, no matter what our inner tribulations or outer experiences. Gurudeva often put this question to us: "Where is your mind? Where is the center of your being?" Thus he reminded us to keep our consciousness always centered within, on God. The constant focus of our being and attention should be the inner peace of God's presence, the feeling that one has after a deep meditation; so pleasant, so peaceful, so at-one with God. No other desire remains, no slightest restlessness ripples the consciousness. This is how man should be all the time. He should not permit anything to ruffle him.

Any disturbance in our lives ought to be viewed as a test of God, meant to instruct and strengthen us. A chain is only as strong as its weakest link; each one of us is only as strong as our greatest weakness. We must learn to stand calm, unshaken, undismayed, no matter what comes in life. That equilibrium of consciousness cannot be attained by merely reading spiritual truths or talking about them, but only by meditation, direct personal communion with God. The older one gets, the more he sees what disappointments life metes out to him; its pleasures do not fulfill their promise. But the more deeply he seeks God, the more he will realize there is nothing that can equal the joy of God's presence. Only that Joy is real in this delusive world of change and relativity. Nothing else man craves can even begin to give such satisfaction.

The Emptiness Only God Can Fill

I saw recently the sad news about the suicide of a successful young actress. She had everything the world thinks it needs to be happy. Yet she had spoken of a great emptiness, a great void, within herself. Why do people feel such a void? Because their attention is too external; they have not anchored it in the peace of God within. "The world is not as it seems," Paramahansaji used to say to us. When we grasp at materiality, its substance disappears within our clasp. The material side of life is just a mass of ephemeral thoughts and impressions, metamorphosing into nothingness. If we build our happiness upon externals alone, we find we have nothing but foam, which slowly melts away. Man feels a tremendous emptiness and loneliness when he has no life with God within.

If man would be truly and lastingly happy in this world, he must build a sound spiritual life within; he must establish a personal relationship with God. This is possible by deep daily meditation, as Paramahansa Yogananda has taught us who follow this path of Self-Realization. And in addition to meditating, constantly take the name of God mentally, throughout the day, repeating it again and again with deep devotion. Sometimes I think of God in the form of Lord Jesus, or Lord Krishna, and I love Him in those forms. Sometimes I conceive of God as my beloved Divine Mother, and I love Him in that form. Sometimes I see the Lord as my Guru, and I love Him in that form. One may visualize God in whatever aspect most rouses one's devotion and keeps his mind inwardly attuned to the Divine. What a tremendous world lies within each one of us!* "My kingdom," said Jesus, "is not of this world."† "My heaven lies within," said Gurudeva. That inner heaven is not a nebulous nothingness; it is real and joyous. Unless and until we have found that heaven within, life for us will be a series of unpleasant upsets.

We might as well accept the fact that so long as we fight for self, or selfishly hold on to anything, sooner or later our peace and that possession will be wrested from us. We should want to receive only that which comes from the hand of the Divine, and we should want to possess it for only as long as it is God's will. We recognize the blessings He sends to us by the sweet peace and joy that fill our being when we receive His gifts, and by the sense of nonattachment we feel while enjoying them.

Begin every day with this thought: "O God, there is nothing I want except to do Your will. There is nothing I am holding on to except You. I seek Your guidance in all things, and I will do my best to follow You." We may not always be able to follow God's will perfectly—when we can, we will no longer be required

* "And when he was demanded of the Pharisees, when the kingdom of God should come, he answered them and said, The kingdom of God cometh not with observation: Neither shall they say, Lo here! or, lo there! for, behold, the kingdom of God is within you" (Luke 17:20–21).

† John 18:36.

to live on this mundane sphere—but each time we fall we should pick ourselves up and try again. We must never grieve over any setback, nor dwell on self-pity, but rather say, "I shall do my best, and I shall never be swayed from my divine goal of striving to please Thee." Like a child, cling to Divine Mother; like a child, surrender to Her. Practice greater faith; cultivate more devotion. These are essential.

The Indian scriptures state that there are two types of devotees, which are described in a charming illustration. One type is said to be like the baby monkey that clings steadfastly to its mother as she swings from one tree to another; it holds on so tightly it never falls. The other kind of devotee is described as like the little kitten that is picked up by its mother and carried from one place to another; the kitten is utterly relaxed, without tension or fear, completely confident no matter where the mother carries or places it. We should be like both types. During times of trouble, when it seems as if we are being tossed from limb to limb, so to speak, we should hold on to the Divine Mother steadfastly like the monkey. At other times we should be like the kitten; utterly content, forgetful of self, in total confident dependence on the Divine Being. Such a devotee knows what real peace is.

Truth Drawn from Within Changes One's Life

Truth is as old as time and as life itself; yet it is ever new. The moment we make it our own it becomes new for us. We may read a truth again and again, without its seeming to hold anything for us personally. We wonder why we are not getting something out of it. The reason is that we have not yet drawn that truth from within ourselves. Truth cannot be grafted onto us from without. It must be brought out from within, or it will ever remain unreal to us. At some time we all have had the experience, while meditating or being otherwise spiritually attuned, of instantly understanding some truth we had previously read without recognition. What an exhilarating feeling it is! Suddenly we have brought forth that truth from within ourselves and beheld it clearly for the first time.

All truth lies hidden in the soul, because the soul is a reflection of God, and God is truth. Therefore, we are truth. But so long as we identify with the little ego, fight for selfish ends, and remain bound by our opinions, likes, and dislikes, truth is obscured from us, because we are still clinging to the false notions created by *maya,* delusion. We must pray to Divine Mother to tear away this veil of *maya.* When She does, the experience is sometimes very fierce; we may not like to see the truth about ourselves. But do not fear it. Divine Mother wants only to perfect Her children, and She will send no test that we have not the strength within to face and conquer.

Above all, cry night and day for devotion for God, that you may find that One Love. Every soul is crying for love, for understanding, companionship, comfort. Wise is the man who seeks them from God. That devotee is the one who gets out of this ocean of suffering by reaching the shores of peace, joy, wisdom, and love divine. That is where we are all headed, but so many waste time and energy swimming in meaningless circles.

Whatever peace, joy, or devotion you gather in your heart from meditation, hold on to it; jealously, zealously, protect it, and strive to build upon it. The way to do this is to practice *japa yoga,* taking the name of God as often as you can in the midst of the activities and demands of your daily duties. If we lived only according to Paramahansa Yogananda's poem, "God! God! God!" we would know what God is. In every phase of our lives—in our work, meditation, struggling with difficulties, enjoying simple pleasures—we must continually be anchored inwardly in the thought: "God! God! God!"

God Is with Us Always

The way to catch God is to remember God, because He is never away from us. He has been with us since the beginning of our creation; and He will be with us always. It is we who are away from Him, because our minds are too busy with other things and with fighting for the little self: "I am hurt, I am sad, I am misunderstood, I am unloved." We are not this body and ego; but we have identified ourselves with the emotions, habits, and limited consciousness of the ego. We are children of God, made in His blissful image. Never be satisfied until you can feel this more and more in your life.

When your life is dull or unhappy it is because you have given insufficient attention to God; you have had too much consciousness of worry and material concerns, and not enough meditation. There is nothing in this world more entertaining, more intoxicating, more blissful, more satisfying, than God—the Beloved Mother, Father, Divine Being, Friend. He is our one and only True Love.

Thou Shalt Have No Other Gods

Self-Realization Fellowship Ashram Center, Encinitas, California, June 21, 1972

We often fail to appreciate what God has given us. On my visit to the foothills of the Himalayas, I noticed that the natives who live on the very threshold of those magnificent mountains—the most beautiful in the world—take them for granted. Tourists experienced overwhelming awe, yet there was no corresponding exaltation in the minds of the residents.

One of the great delights of this world consists in never getting too used to anything, so that we can always find something new, inspiring, and thrilling about our life. I have never come to Encinitas or entered the grounds of Mt. Washington without feeling a great thrill, as if I were beholding them for the first time. Practice this ideal of not taking anything or anyone for granted.

Those who enjoy life most have the ability to appreciate their environment, the people among whom they live, everything God gives. This ability comes when we try every day to practice the presence of God, because He is ever new. I remember Master's saying many times that the romance with God is the most sublime experience in the world, greater than any other relationship the soul can experience, because His love, communion with Him, is always ever new. The relationship with God never grows stale; there is always some fresh delight or experience, some unsuspected awareness or unfolding of wisdom and understanding, some unknown thrill of devotion that touches the devotee's heart.

One of the vital points on the spiritual path is to see every day as a new beginning. And above all in importance is practicing God's presence from the moment we awaken in the morning until we fall asleep at night. That was the training Guruji gave; he didn't place first the external things in life, or the building of an organization.

How many times, when one of us might comment upon having some particular problem, Master's guidance was simply: "Do your best, and give it to God," or "Keep your mind more on God." The more you put your mind on God, the more you will find it possible to cope with all of life's experiences, whether they be negative or positive.

In 1936, when Guruji returned from India, he said to us: "I seek no power; I seek nothing, for I have given all to Divine Mother. I have cast my desires into the flame of one desire: to behold my Divine Mother's face. On the altar of my heart I have burned all lesser desires. One glimpse of Her face, one glimpse of that mighty Light, is all I seek."

That is the way Paramahansaji lived, and the ideal he is still striving to instill in all. He said: "I am not bound by this body. Someday, when my body will be no more, I shall be happy to watch you from Spirit. I shall see how you are growing spiritually, and how this work of the Gurus is unfolding. I am the ever-living Spirit, undying; and I shall be watching over you with a million eyes."

If from this day forward you hold on to the one thought, "I have given all my desires into the one desire for Divine Mother," and again and again bring your consciousness back to it, you will find life takes on a totally new meaning, and gives fresh inspiration to you every day.

Gurudeva used to say: "My interest is to strive to awaken in every soul who crosses my path the one desire to commune with God." This is the meaning of Self-realization: the ability to commune directly with God. It can be done, not by keeping our consciousness always involved in the five senses, in perceiving this external world, but by shutting off the sense telephones and learning to commune with God in the temple of silence within.

The Scripture says: "Thou shalt have no other gods before Me. . . . I the Lord thy God am a jealous God."* The Lord wasn't saying this to renunciants only; He was speaking to all mankind, all His children. He was being quite realistic. He meant: "My dears, I have given you reason, intelligence, discrimination, and the voice of conscience to show you the difference between right and wrong. I have done everything I can to help you become a happy individual reflecting divinity, My image within you. Now, live your life. Pursue what you want, but do not forget Me. When you divorce yourself from Me, from the One who has given you life, who has instilled in you divine qualities, you lose your way."

* Exodus 20:3, 5.

Then God is no longer first in your life; you have put other things in *His* place.

When we express anger, greed—any of the qualities that we do not admire in man—we have put God out of our lives. But when we try to the very best of our ability to express the hidden Divinity that is within us, we place God first. Only then does man find his own Self. That man truly lives who awakens with the dawn and is filled with life, the joy of living, the desire to forget himself and express his greater Self, which is God within him. Until then he is merely existing.

Guruji goes on to say: "The way to God is through continuous practice of His presence every moment of your existence, and by daily deep meditation. When with the shells of your yearning you shall break the ramparts of silence behind which God is hiding, the divine Being will be caught within your heart."

The Value of Silence

In our ashrams, the devotees are encouraged to practice silence. It is a vital part of one's *sadhana* or search for God; because if we don't learn a little bit about observing silence we never really know what it is to listen for the voice of God. It is very difficult to know God unless one puts into effect good habits; and learning to control one's speech is an essential.

Guruji was very much opposed to gossip, absolutely intolerant of it. He considered it one of the most vicious, cruel habits indulged in by mankind. To persons who came to him with gossip he often said: "I have heard your unkind words about others. Now I want you to talk against yourself. Bring to my attention your faults, because you have them also."

Guruji gave a beautiful illustration: "This little mouth we have is like a cannon, and words are the ammunition. They destroy many things. Do not talk uselessly, and not until you think your words are going to do some good."

In many religions you will find those who observe silence. In India they call it *mauna,* and one who practices it, a *muni*. Every devotee who would know God should set aside some portion of every day to practice this marvelous quality. It can be done if we make up our minds we want to do it.

"The great man," said Guruji, "talks very little; but when he speaks, people listen." It's true; you will never find a great man who is very talkative. He is inclined to be rather silent, to be more involved in listening than in talking. But when he does speak, all listen.

Yoga Teaches Man to Change Himself

Guruji goes on to say: "We must never concentrate on others' faults. . . . 'Judge not, that ye be not judged.'* That is the illusion, to be interested in others' mistakes when we have plenty of cleaning to do in our own mental home. First, clean your own home."

The devotee who would know God should learn to be more silent, and to listen to the voice of Love within. He should learn to live love in his life, to practice it first within his heart, and then express it outwardly.

How many times in our lives we hurt people by our words and actions. This is what is called mental cruelty; it is worse in many ways than physical brutality. Never say anything under the emotion of meanness. Better to

* Matthew 7:1.

"zip the lip" if you cannot speak with a heart that is free from meanness. The desire to hurt someone—child, husband, parents—is brutal!

The science of yoga helps man to overcome frailties. It teaches him to change himself, his everyday habits, so that he becomes a better individual, not merely what is called a "street angel and a house devil"—one who speaks beautifully before others, but is not that kind of person in his own home. Yoga teaches the individual to introspect—as Robert Burns says, to "see ourselves as others see us."* Yoga gives one that power. It trains the devotee to see himself as others see him, not as he thinks he is; there is a vast difference between the two.

"What am I? Am I mean? Do I take pleasure in hurting people, in talking against others? If so, I had better learn to overcome these ugly habits." This is what is meant by introspection.

The very first *sloka* of the Gita says (symbolically): "Gathered together on the battlefield of my consciousness are my good qualities and my evil qualities. How did I fare this day? Which conquered?"† Was I calm in the midst of upheaval? Was my speech kind when I wanted rather to say something mean in order to hurt somebody? Was I unselfish, or did I take the best for myself?

* "Oh, wad some power the giftie gie us/To see oursels as others see us!"

† "Gathered together on the sacred bodily tract—the field of good and evil actions—what did my opposing tendencies do? Which side won today in the ceaseless struggle? All my children—the crooked, tempting, evil tendencies, and the opposing forces of self-discipline and discrimination—come now, tell me, what did they do?" (Bhagavad Gita I:1).

Live love within. When you want to do or say something unkind, think love in your heart. And then express it outwardly by some kind act or deed.

Become like a flower; if you pick a beautiful rose and crush it in your hands, it gives off a sweet fragrance. That's the way a devotee of God should be. No matter how he is crushed by unkindness from anyone, he gives off the sweet fragrance of forgiveness, of kindness. That is the way St. Francis was. All saints express compassion and kindness.

The divine man doesn't try to justify himself. Great peace comes to such a soul. He is more immersed in what God thinks of him than in what man thinks. God is the first love in his life; he puts no other gods before Him. Guruji said: "If all the world honors you and God does not, you are indeed poor; because one day, when the signal is given for you to depart from this fleshly house, you will have to leave everything. But if you have the recognition of God, you have everything; for you take His recognition with you to the great beyond."

The divine man is concerned with his own right behavior toward other people. "Do I give kindness, think kindness, speak kindness? Do I do good in this world?" He is not interested in being a great teacher in order to do good. No. Wherever he is, whatever he is, he wants only to do good. That individual is like the fragrant flower; devotee-bees gather around him.

This is another illustration Guruji used to give: "Flies love to swarm around filthy things. The bee wants only to go where it can collect sweet nectar. I don't like to see people behave like flies, gathering wherever there is ugliness, gossip, unkindness, meanness, hatred, jealousy, envy, bigotry, and prejudice. I would rather see a garden of fragrant flowering soul qualities where human bees are attracted to sip the divine honey of love and compassion and kindness."

When I say these words every one of you responds. Why? Because they express the very nature of your soul; and I am merely reminding you of what you are, souls made in the image of the One Beloved.

"Thou shalt have no other gods before Me. . . . I the Lord thy God am a jealous God"; now you understand better what the Lord means: When we do Godlike things, when we express Godlike qualities, which are innate within every one of us, we have no other gods—jealousy, greed, anger, hatred, or anything else—we have made Him, His qualities, His ideals, first in our lives.

An Experience with Divine Mother

This is something so beautiful, about an experience of Master's here in Encinitas. He said: "While others waste their time, meditate, and you will see that in meditation that Silence will speak to you. 'Give my Mother a soul call. She can't remain hidden anymore. Come out of the silent sky, come out of the mountain glen, come out of my secret soul, come out of my cave of silence.'* Everywhere I see the Divine Spirit manifesting in form as the Mother. Water condensed becomes ice, and so invisible Spirit can be frozen into form by my devotion's frost. If only you could see the beautiful eyes of the Mother that I beheld last night. My heart is filled with joy eternal. The little cup of my heart cannot hold the joy and the love

* From *Cosmic Chants*.

that I beheld in those eyes—looking at me, sometimes smiling. I said to Her, 'Oh! and people call You unreal!' and Divine Mother smiled. 'It is You who are real and all things else are unreal,' I said, and the Divine Mother smiled again. I prayed, 'O Mother, be Thou real unto all.' And I wrote Her name on the foreheads of a few who were present. Satan will never be able to take over their lives."

Some may wonder why Guruji referred to God as Divine Mother. On some occasions he referred to God as Father, on others as Mother. In the ultimate sense God is formless, but the devotee may choose to worship any aspect of God that appeals to him. Sometimes we like to think of God as absolute Spirit, but most of the time mankind prefers to think of God with form. For many lives we have been encased in form, so we cannot help but think of God in terms of having characteristic features. Since the beginning of history man has encased the Absolute in some image. This is not idol worship. We put Christ Consciousness in the beautiful figure of Jesus, but the Infinite is not limited to that. Why is it that when we look at an image of Jesus, many of us feel upliftment? We remember his compassion and forgiveness, his marvelous quality of love for mankind. We might not feel it so much if we didn't see the form.

Guruji goes on to say: "Such joy I feel day and night. Day passes into night and I forget time entirely. I don't have to meditate now, because That which I meditated upon has become one with me. Sometimes I breathe, sometimes I don't breathe. Sometimes the heart beats, sometimes it doesn't. I see that I have dropped everything except that one consciousness. Whether this physical engine is running or not, I behold that great light of God.

Such is my joy." This is the ultimate goal everyone who ever communed with God experiences. He finds that though he resides in a physical form, his consciousness is expanded beyond form.

Last, let me read to you this thought of Guruji's: "Even if God were to send ten thousand Jesus Christs to redeem you, you cannot be redeemed unless you yourself make the effort. No great soul can help you unless you help yourself. Divine law has no limitations. You are already the child of God. Make the effort, have the knowledge of the law of God, and meditate daily; you will reach your divine goal. Meditate morning and evening. Go deeper and deeper in meditation. And meditate late at night, and into the night. Don't think you must have so much sleep." This is true. Any of you who have meditated very deeply know that in deep meditation the body and mind have complete rest, far greater than you can have in the subconscious realm of sleep. In sleep we dream, we don't always have rest for the body or the mind. But in deep meditation the body and mind enter a state of total tranquillity, total peace.

If you really want God, you must plunge deeply into the desire for God. Love Him with all your heart. Prove to God that you want Him, nothing less. Seek God, because so long as you do not know that you are one with Him, you are bound by this world of duality, this world of suffering. God doesn't cause mankind this suffering. We are part and parcel of Him, and unless we realize this we will never be happy. We suffer because we have separated ourselves from Him. We feel loneliness, we feel insecurity; we tremble when something happens to this mortal form because we do not see the unbroken circle of our existence, which is infinite. All suffering is a result of thinking of ourselves as this fleshly form. Whether the suffering be fear of poverty, of ill health, or of the unknown, it is the result of our not knowing God.

When one begins to realize himself as the immortal soul, he knows that fire cannot burn, nor water drown, nor bullets shatter it.* That is what Yoga and religion are all about: to help man realize his immortal, eternal, indestructible nature. Truth is marvelous. You can talk about it endlessly, and you can sum it up in just a few words: Truth is that which helps and encourages every human being to make his way back to God.

God has no favorites. He loves each one of us as He loves His greatest saints. The only difference between ordinary men and the saints is that the saints never gave up trying. As often as they fell they picked themselves up saying, "Never mind, I'll go on trying. I am determined to find Truth, Love, Wisdom. I am determined to find God."

That must be your goal also. Thou shalt have no other gods. While seeking God inwardly, express your search for God outwardly by serving Him every day of your life in whatever ways you see open to you.

Remember that God is as close to you as your thought allows Him to be. He is omnipresent. If at this moment you accept that He is with you, just behind your closed eyes, you will feel His nearness. Meditate upon it, and you will find it will come to pass in your life.

* "No weapon can pierce the soul; no fire can burn it; no water can moisten it; nor can any wind wither it" (Bhagavad Gita II:23).

Experiences with My Guru, Paramahansa Yogananda

Reminiscences drawn from talks in India and America

Every human heart craves love. And all forms of human love—that between parents and children, husband and wife, master and servant, friend and friend, guru and disciple—come from the One Love, which is God.

Every human heart is also seeking happiness. It is the goal of life. One may say, "My goal is success in business," or "My goal is to create beautiful music"; but through the fulfillment of every specific desire we are hoping, even if only subconsciously, to attain happiness. The desire to be happy, and to love and be loved, are the motivating forces behind all our activities and ambitions.

The sages of India have said that God is ever-existing, ever-conscious, ever-new Bliss. They tell us that the happiness we seek, the joy that will endure forever and never grow stale, is to be found in God. And where is He? His divine image resides in every human being as the soul. We do not know the divine peace of soul-realization because we have turned our attention and our seeking toward things of this world. We should remember that the happiness attainable on earth is conditional and fleeting. Only God's bliss is eternal.

Love and joy, in their purest forms, can be found only in God. But we seek them everywhere else instead. Only when confronted with severe trials and much sorrow do we begin to think of God and start devoting a little time to worship—prayer or *puja* or the recitation of a *mantram*. But the time comes when such outer observances do not satisfy us. If the mind is wandering hither and thither, prayer is ineffective, and the repetition of *mantrams* and practice of *japa* fail to bring the response from God that the soul craves.

God Can Be Known Only Through Personal Experience

There is a fruit of great sweetness called cherimoya. It is round, with a green skin; the inside is a soft white pulp, throughout which are large black seeds. I have described this fruit to you, but do you actually know what a cherimoya is and how it tastes? Not if you have only heard my description of it, but have never seen or eaten the fruit.

So it is with the Lord. Saints and *rishis** have described their experiences of God, but the mere reading of their accounts will not enable you to know Him. We cannot realize God merely through a description given to us by others. We ourselves must experience His presence in the great state of ecstasy that comes from prolonged and deep meditation.

The ordinary man is always so busy with worries, responsibilities, and desires for worldly pleasures that he never turns his mind to God. And even if he does

* God-realized sages.

set aside a little time each day to give his attention to the Lord and to seek peace within, he is unsuccessful in his meditation because he does not meditate deeply enough.

All Devotion Offered to Guru Is Given to God

In *sadhana* a guru is necessary. The mind of a true guru is always anchored and absorbed in the Cosmic Beloved. Whether he follows the path of *Raja, Jnana, Karma,* or *Bhakti Yoga,** his consciousness is one with God. All devotion offered the guru by his disciples he gives to the Lord. He directs the devotee's mind not to himself, but to the Heavenly Father.

Such a great one was my divine guru, Paramahansa Yogananda. He wished his disciples never to become attached to or dependent on his personality. He wanted us to love and to seek the Lord alone. He always turned our thoughts to God, and trained us to keep our minds attuned night and day to Him. Whenever Gurudeva saw our minds becoming absorbed in anything external, he scolded us. He taught us to keep our minds always drunk with the thought of God, our lips always speaking of Him, our hearts ever singing to Him. In Gurudeva we had before us a true example of how one's whole being should be absorbed in the Divine.

An Experience in Nirbikalpa Samadhi

The last period of Guruji's life was lived in the unbroken ecstasy of God, or *nirbikalpa samadhi,*† which

* The "royal," discriminative, serviceful, and devotional approaches to God, respectively.

† *Samadhi* is a blissful superconscious state in which a yogi perceives the unity of individualized soul and Cosmic Spirit. *Nirbikalpa samadhi*

began in June 1948. I, along with a few others, was privileged to be present at the time he entered this state. It was toward evening, and he had called us to come to his room. He was sitting in a large chair and was just about to eat a mango. Suddenly his mind was sucked within in ecstasy; he remained all night in *samadhi*. Witnessing it was an amazing and transforming experience. We had of course seen him in *samadhi* before, but during this particular experience a great miracle occurred: Gurudeva posed questions to the Divine Mother, and She then used his voice to reply. Many predictions that the Divine Mother made through Guruji that night about world affairs and about the spread of the Self-Realization message have since come to pass.

I had often been a "doubting Thomas," wanting definite proof of the existence of God. That night all doubt was removed forever. My consciousness was set afire with love and longing for the Divine Beloved whose voice we heard and whose love we felt through our blessed Guru.

After that *samadhi* Guruji told us: "I don't know what Divine Mother will do with my life. Either She will take me away from this earth or She wants me to withdraw from organizational work and remain in seclusion." Guruji went to a retreat in the desert, and from that time on he remained for the most part in seclusion, devoting himself to meditation and writing.

---

is the highest state of ecstasy, experienced only by the most advanced masters. The physical immobility and trance condition that characterize the lesser states of *samadhi* are not requisite in the *nirbikalpa* state. A master in this highest ecstasy can continue to perform all normal and exacting activities with no loss of God-perception within.

Last Days with the Guru

In the last week of February 1952 Guruji received word at the desert that he had been invited to speak in Los Angeles at a reception for the Ambassador of India, Sri Binay Ranjan Sen. Gurudeva returned to our headquarters in Los Angeles on March 1. On March 3, under Guruji's direction, we spent many hours preparing special sweetmeats and curries for the Ambassador, who was to be a guest at Self-Realization Fellowship headquarters the following day.

Late that night, when the preparations neared completion, the blessed Master asked me to walk with him down the hall. He stopped and sat by the picture of his guru, Swami Sri Yukteswarji, and spoke so lovingly of that great soul who had guided his steps to God.

Then Gurudeva said to me, "Do you realize that it is just a matter of hours before I leave this body?" A great pain of sadness went through my heart. Not long before, when Gurudeva had spoken of leaving his body soon, I had said to him, "Master, what will we do without you? You are the diamond in the ring of our hearts and of your society. Of what value is the setting without the beauty of the diamond?" Then came the answer from the great *bhakta:** "Remember this: When I am gone, only love can take my place. Be absorbed night and day in the love of God, and give that love to all."

For lack of such love, the world has become full of miseries.

On the last day (March 7), when I came into Master's room he was sitting very quietly in lotus posture on his reclining chair. When I went over to him, he

* Lover of God.

put his fingers to his lips, indicating he wished silence to be observed. His mind was very much withdrawn, absorbed in God. The room emanated a powerful divine vibration of peace and love. In the evening he went to the Biltmore Hotel where the reception for the Ambassador was to be held. That night Guruji spoke with such quiet fervor of love for God that the whole audience was lifted to another plane of consciousness. Surely they had never before heard anyone speak so intimately of the presence of the Lord.

Many years before, Master had predicted, "When I depart from this body, I will leave it speaking of God and my beloved India." And so on this night our Guru's last words on earth were of God and India. He quoted from his poem, *My India:* "Where Ganges, woods, Himalayan caves, and men dream God—I am hallowed; my body touched that sod." With these words, he lifted his eyes to the *kutastha* center* and slowly slipped to the floor.

In an instant some of us were by his side. He had taught us to chant *Aum* in his ear to bring him out of *samadhi;* Ananda Mata† and I bent over our divine Guru and began to chant *Aum*. As I did so, a great peace and joy suddenly descended on me, and I felt a tremendous spiritual force enter my body. The blessing received that night has never left me.

The disciple must strive to keep mental and spir-

* The center of divine awareness or Christ Consciousness, located between the eyebrows.

† A faithful disciple of Paramahansa Yogananda since 1931, and sister of Sri Daya Mata. Ananda Mata entered the ashram in 1933 at the age of 17. She is an officer and member of the Board of Directors of SRF/YSS.

itual attunement with the guru. The power of the blessing of a God-realized guru is incomparable.

Follow the Sadhana of the Guru

The *sadhana* taught by our gurudeva, Paramahansa Yogananda, shows us how to apply the "Eightfold Path of Yoga" outlined by the sage Patanjali. First comes *yama-niyama,* the moral and spiritual precepts all men must follow in order to lead a life in harmony with divine law. Then comes *asana* or right posture for meditation, with the spine held straight. Right *asana* is important to prevent the body from distracting the mind as it seeks to go Godward.

Then comes *pranayama,* or life-force control, which is necessary so that the breath does not keep the consciousness tied to the body. Next, interiorization of the mind, or *pratyahara,* frees us from worldly distractions that reach us through the five senses. Then we are free for concentration and meditation, *dharana* and *dhyana,* which lead to *samadhi:* the superconscious experience of oneness with God.

The Lord has no favorites; He loves all equally. The sun shines the same on the charcoal and on the diamond, but the diamond receives and reflects the light. Most persons have "charcoal" mentalities; that is why they think that God does not bless them. The love and blessings are there; man has only to receive them. Through *bhakti* he can transform his consciousness into a diamond mentality to receive and reflect fully the love and grace of God. Then he will have peace and fulfillment in his life. Just a little meditation and sincere love for our Divine Creator will bring peace into the hearts of men, and then world conditions will truly improve.

By giving our hearts' devotion to the guru, and by receiving the guru's unconditional divine love and friendship in return, we learn what it is to love God sincerely. The guru awakens within us true love for God, and teaches us how to love Him.

The Path of Devotion

Self-Realization Fellowship international headquarters, Los Angeles, California, April 13, 1965

The easiest way to find God is through devotion. Any person seeking the easy way should concentrate predominantly upon developing this quality. But along with devotion he will also need to develop discrimination. Our guru, Paramahansa Yogananda, once defined discrimination as learning to do the things we ought to do when we ought to do them.

Spiritual discrimination keeps our thoughts one-pointed. Whenever we perform any action, such discrimination makes us ask ourselves: "Will this give me greater awareness of God?" It enables us to say "*neti, neti* ('not this, not this')" to those actions that will not lead to Him, and vow to avoid them. To those activities that discrimination tells us will lead to God we can say, "This I will faithfully do." If you follow these two basic principles, devotion plus discrimination, you will see that they constitute the simplest way to find God. Naturally, when I say "devotion," that includes practice of the guru-given techniques of meditation.

What is the easiest way to win anyone? Not through reason; through love. So the logical way to win the Divine Friend is to love Him. Love is what I was looking for in this world. I lived for love. But I wanted love that was perfect; and I realized that we have no right to expect perfect love from human beings, because they themselves are imperfect. One trouble with the world today is that husbands and wives, children, families, complain of the lack of love they receive from one another. They do not stop to think that if you want love, you must first *give* love. You can't get love by just demanding it from someone. You must give, and then you will receive.

And if you want God, you must first give love to Him. You will receive in return such abundance that you will no longer cry for the imperfect love of this world.

Whenever I would read about ideal love between friends, or parents and children, or husbands and wives I would think: "Beloved God, if these human relationships can be so beautiful, how much more beautiful must be the relationship with You, from whom these different forms of love flow?" How inspiring and encouraging is that thought! But you cannot find God merely by thus reasoning about His qualities; you have to try to feel them, to concentrate on them, to meditate upon His nature, until the qualities He manifests become part of your own experience. To know God as love, take a particular thought that rouses devotion in you and dwell on it for a long time during deep meditation to increase the depth of your feeling.

Devotion Should Be for God Alone, Not to Impress Others

The devotee who follows the path of *bhakti,* or devotion, may pass through a stage of emotionalism for a while. But if he is deeply sincere, that outward fervor will gradually pass, and in its place will be a deep inner devotional state of consciousness. You have read about this in the lives of many saints who followed the path of *bhakti.* There is a period of great emotionalism; tears flow and the devotee sometimes even loses consciousness. But if he perseveres and is deeply sincere, if he is not trying to impress others, gradually his mind becomes so absorbed within that there is very little outward display of his feelings.

Some seekers, experiencing a little devotion, make much show of it in the presence of others with the conscious or subconscious wish to impress them. Through such external display, they lose all of their true devotional feeling. When one goes into that initial emotional stage, he should ask himself, "Am I being sincere?" Always remember that. The devotee should honestly analyze himself: "Am I trying to impress someone? Am I as deeply emotional in my feeling for God when I am alone, where no one can watch me, as I am with others?" That is the first thing he should do: be honest with himself. If he finds that his feelings are just as deep, that the tears flow just as freely when he is alone, then his devotion is on the right track. If, on the other hand, he finds that his emotion is much stronger when he is with others, he should mentally stand aside for a moment and ask himself if in fact he is really hoping to impress those around him with his "great spiritual advancement." If he finds that this is so he should get busy and deeply pray to God, "O Lord, please do not let me desecrate this spark of devotion I feel for You! Help me to remove this outward show, that none may see my love for You. Let me keep it hidden, sacred between Thee and me." In this manner he should reverse his outflowing thoughts and feelings and take them within.

When the devotee sincerely loves God, when his devotion becomes deep and pure, he forgets the world. He no longer cares whether the world thinks him a madman or a saint, whether the world accepts or rejects him. He wants only to feel the love of God, and to be absorbed in that love. In that consciousness, when the tears may sometimes trickle down his cheeks, if his mind happens to go outward for a moment, his desire is that no one see those tears but God. That devotee may know he is on the right path; and that gradually his devotion will become deeper, more withdrawn, more inward—but even then, it may once in a while take an outward turn.

Bliss Is the Ultimate Goal of Man

Man is both a reasoning and a loving being. In his soul are both reason and feeling, and each is intoxicating. I remember our Guru's once saying, "When I am in the wisdom state, reason is uppermost and I am not conscious of devotion. When I am in the state of devotion, that is uppermost and I feel reason less." But both love and wisdom give the intoxication of divine bliss.

Every human being is seeking bliss. It is the only goal of life. And that is what God is—ever-existing, ever-new, ever-conscious bliss. It is also the nature of the soul. You may say that man seeks many different things. But from all of them, from the fulfillment of his search, he hopes for just one experience: joy, or bliss. If he seeks love, it is not because he wants sorrow; he wants to experience the joy of being loved. If he seeks wisdom, it is not because he wants limitation; he wants the intoxicating joy that comes from being all-knowing. Why does man seek gold? Gold, or money, in itself has no meaning. Man seeks it for the joy of fulfillment that comes with having everything he wants. When he seeks fame, it is for the joy of feeling, "I am all powerful," or "I am eternal." In his every search the ultimate goal of man is bliss.

The nature of the soul is power, bliss, love, eternal consciousness, omniscience, omnipresence. And so in all of the things man seeks in this world, he is trying to experience those qualities that are a part of his true nature. Analyze it; what is fame but the desire for immortality, to be known while we're here, and to go on living in memory after we're gone from this world. Man runs after these things because he is unconsciously seeking to experience his own soul nature.

Man is therefore to be forgiven his frantic search for satisfaction in the material life. It is not wrong to seek fulfillment, but the way in which it is sought is often wrong. That which is eternal cannot be found in that which is temporal.

There is only one way to attain absolute satisfaction. Christ knew it, and that is why he said: "But seek ye first the kingdom of God, and His righteousness; and all these things shall be added unto you." If you seek God, you will find in Him all else that you are yearning for. You will realize fulfillment in Him who is eternal, for you will find your eternal Self.

A Blessing from Mahavatar Babaji

Self-Realization Fellowship Ashram Center, Encinitas, California, August 24, 1965

During a visit to Paramahansa Yogananda's ashrams in India (October 1963–May 1964), Sri Daya Mata made a sacred pilgrimage to a Himalayan cave that has been sanctified by the physical presence of Mahavatar Babaji.* For some time afterward, Daya Mata declined in public meetings to speak about her experience. But when, at this *satsanga* in Encinitas, a devotee asked Mataji to tell of her visit to Babaji's cave, the Divine Will prompted a positive response. Following is her account, for the inspiration of all.

There was a very special relationship between Paramahansa Yogananda and Mahavatar Babaji. Gurudeva often spoke of Babaji, and of the occasion in Calcutta, just before Paramahansaji left India to come to

* The supreme Guru in the line of God-realized masters who assume responsibility for the spiritual welfare of all members of Self-Realization Fellowship (Yogoda Satsanga Society of India) who faithfully practice *Kriya Yoga*.

The cave to which Daya Mata made her pilgrimage is the one in which the Mahavatar was staying at the time he bestowed the sacred *Kriya Yoga* on his great disciple Lahiri Mahasaya, in 1861. The wondrous story of their meeting, as related by Lahiri Mahasaya, has been recorded by Paramahansa Yogananda in *Autobiography of a Yogi,*

n deep divine communion at the cave of Mahavatar Babaji, in the Himalayas near Ranikhet, 1963

"The voice of silence spoke loudly of the presence of the Divine. Waves of realization poured through my consciousness; and the prayers I offered that day have since been answered."

PARAMAHANSA YOGANANDA
Founder

SELF-REALIZATION FELLOWSHIP

International Headquarters

PUBLISHERS
Inner Culture Magazine
Now EAST-WEST

3880 SAN RAFAEL AVENUE • MOUNT WASHINGTON ESTATES • LOS ANGELES 31, CALIF.

Letter from Paramahansaji to Daya Mata on her birthday, January 31, 1946

"Many years God has travelled us together working for Him. Your birth has been important in the family of SRF and the family and parents who brought you up. Your sincere joyous intelligent service to SRF and to God has been extremely pleasing to me. May you be born in the Cosmic Mother and inspire all with your spiritual motherliness only—only to bring others to God by the example of your life. Happy Birthday to you. Blessings eternal."

Daya Mataji's favorite photograph of Paramahansa Yogananda

"...his duty as the guru was to help the disciple to recognize and overcome delusion; his mission was not merely to increase man's intellectual knowledge about God, but to lead souls to Him."

Satsanga in Paris during three-month tour of SRF European centers, 1969

"Our duty as children of God in this world . . . is to seek understanding: understanding of self, of others, of life, and, above all, of God. This world can be a better place only when understanding reigns in the heart and mind of man."

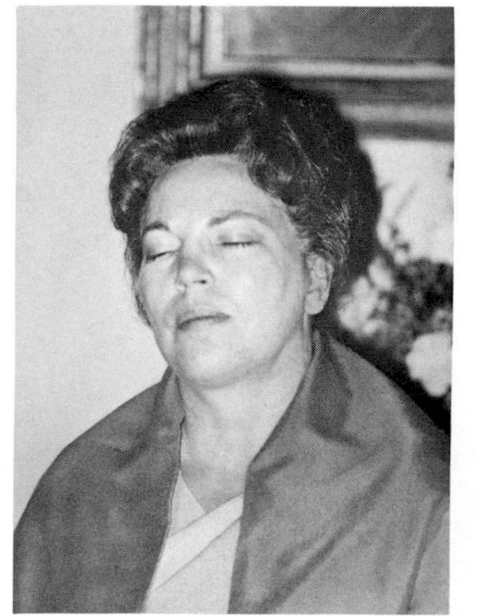

Meditation during *Kriya Yoga* ceremony, SRF international headquarters, Los Angeles, 1965

"Learn to be more silent, and to listen to the voice of Love within."

this country, when the Mahavatar had appeared to him.* Whenever Master referred to the great *avatar,*† it was with such devotion, such a feeling of reverence, that our hearts were filled with divine love and yearning. I sometimes felt that my heart would burst.

After Guruji's passing, the thought of Babaji continued to grow stronger in my consciousness. I used to wonder why, with all due love and reverence for our other beloved *paramgurus,*‡ there was a special feeling in my heart for Babaji; I was not aware of any particular response from him that might have stirred in me this marked sense of closeness to him. Considering myself wholly unworthy, I never expected to have a personal experience of Babaji's holy presence. I thought that perhaps in some future life this blessing might come to me. Never have I asked for or craved spiritual experiences. I only want to love God and to feel His love. My joy comes from being in love with Him; I seek no other reward in life.

---

chapter 34: "During a ramble one early afternoon, I was astounded to hear a distant voice calling my name. I continued my vigorous upward climb....I finally reached a small clearing whose sides were dotted with caves. On one of the rocky ledges stood a smiling young man, extending his hand in welcome....'Lahiri, you have come! Rest here in this cave. It was I who called you.'" The story continues with Lahiri Mahasaya's description of the extraordinary circumstances under which he received from the Mahavatar the sacred *diksha* (initiation) in *Kriya Yoga*.

* See *Autobiography of a Yogi,* chapter 37.

† Divine incarnation: one who has voluntarily returned to earth to help mankind after he himself has attained liberation and full identity with Spirit.

‡ *Paramguru,* guru of one's guru; here referring to the sacred line of Gurus of Self-Realization Fellowship: Mahavatar Babaji, Lahiri Mahasaya, Swami Sri Yukteswar, and Paramahansa Yogananda.

When we went to India this last time, two of the devotees* with me expressed a wish to visit Babaji's cave. At first I felt no deep personal desire to do so, but we made inquiry. The cave is in the Himalayan foothills beyond Ranikhet, near the border of Nepal. Officials in Delhi told us that the northern border areas were closed to foreigners; it seemed that such a trip would be impossible. I was not disappointed. I have seen too many miracles to doubt that Divine Mother has the power to bring about anything She wills. And if She did not will that the trip be made, I had no personal wish in the matter.

A day or two later, Yogacharya Binay Narayan† told me he had been in touch with the Chief Minister of Uttar Pradesh, the state in which Babaji's cave is located. The Chief Minister had given special permission for our party to visit the area. Within two days we were ready for the trip. We didn't have any warm clothing suitable for the colder climate of the mountains, only our cotton saris, and woolen *chuddars* (shawls) to wrap around our shoulders. In our eagerness we were a little foolhardy!

We entrained for Lucknow, capital of the state of Uttar Pradesh, arriving about eight o'clock in the evening at the home of the Governor. We took our meal with him, along with the Chief Minister and other guests. By ten o'clock we were on a train headed for Katgodam, accompanied by the Chief Minister. It was almost dawn

* Ananda Mata and Uma Mata, members of the board of Self-Realization Fellowship/Yogoda Satsanga Society of India.

† Later known as Swami Shyamananda. He was general secretary of Yogoda Satsanga Society of India, an office he held until his passing in 1971.

when we arrived at the little station. From there we had yet to travel by car to the hill station of Dwarahat, where there are accommodations for pilgrims such as we.

A Divine Confirmation from Babaji

For a time I sat in the Katgodam railroad station all alone. The other devotees had gone outside to wait for the cars. With deep feeling and devotion, I was practicing what we call in India *Japa Yoga,* repeating the name of the Divine again and again and again. In this practice, the whole consciousness gradually becomes absorbed in one thought to the exclusion of everything else. I was taking the name of Babaji. All I could think about was Babaji. My heart was bursting with a thrill indescribable.

Suddenly, I lost all awareness of this world. My mind was completely withdrawn into another state of consciousness. In an ecstasy of sweetest joy I beheld the presence of Babaji. I understood what Saint Teresa of Avila meant when she spoke of "seeing" the formless Christ: the individuality of Spirit manifesting as soul, cloaked only in the thought-essence of being. This "seeing" is a perception more vivid and exact in detail than the gross outlines of material forms, or even of visions. Inwardly I bowed and took the dust of his feet.*

Master had told some of us: "You need never concern yourselves about the leadership of our Society. Babaji has already selected those who are destined to lead this work." When I was chosen by the board, I

* An Indian custom, in which one touches the feet of a master, then one's forehead, signifying humility before his spiritual greatness. (Cf. Mark 5:27–34.)

questioned, "Why me?"* Now I found myself appealing to Babaji about it: "They chose me. I am so unworthy. How could it be?" I was sobbing inwardly at his feet.

So sweetly, he replied: "My child, you must not doubt your Guru. He spoke the truth. What he told you is true." As Babaji spoke these words, a blissful peace came over me. My whole being remained bathed in that peace, for how long I do not know.

Gradually I became aware that the others in the party had come back into the room. When I opened my eyes, I beheld my surroundings with a new perception. I remember exclaiming, "Of course! I have been here before." Everything was instantly familiar to me, memories of a past lifetime reawakened!

The cars that were to take us up the hill were ready. We got in and traveled up the winding mountain road. Every sight, every scene I beheld, was familiar to me. After the experience at Katgodam, Babaji's presence remained so strong with me that everywhere I looked, he seemed to be there. We stopped briefly at Ranikhet,

* On one occasion, Paramahansa Yogananda was asked about the appointing of future presidents of Self-Realization Fellowship/ Yogoda Satsanga Society of India, who by virtue of their office would represent him as the spiritual head of SRF/YSS as well. He replied: "There will always be at the head of this organization men and women of realization. They are already known to God and the Gurus."

Though Paramahansaji had chosen and trained Daya Mataji for her future spiritual role, she never inwardly took the appointment literally, feeling that when the time actually came the Lord would surely choose another in her stead. But neither the will of God nor the express wish of Guru was to be altered by this vain hope of one so wholly qualified, but humbly reluctant. *(Publisher's Note)* where we were received by officials of the town who had been notified of our visit by the Chief Minister.

Finally we arrived at the remote little village of Dwarahat, perched high in the Himalayan foothills. We settled in a government rest house, a simple little bungalow for pilgrims. That night many people came from the surrounding countryside to see us. They had heard of the pilgrims from the West who had come to visit the holy cave. Many people in this region talk about Babaji, whose name means "Revered Father." They plied us with questions, and we had *satsanga* together, just as we are having now. Many of them understood English, and someone nearby translated for those who didn't.

A Prophetic Vision

After *satsanga* was over and the villagers had dispersed, we sat for meditation and then retired, climbing into our warm sleeping bags. In the middle of the night I had a superconscious experience. A huge black cloud suddenly swept over me, trying to engulf me. As it did so, I cried out to God, awakening Ananda Ma and Uma Ma, who were in the room with me. They were alarmed and wanted to know what had happened. "I don't want to talk about it now," I told them. "I am all right. Go back to sleep." Through the practice of meditation, the all-knowing power of intuition develops in each one of us. I had intuitively understood what the Divine was telling me through this symbolic experience. It foretold a serious illness I was soon to undergo; and it also indicated that all mankind would face a very dark time during which the evil force would seek to engulf the world. Because the cloud did not completely envelop me—it was repulsed by my thoughts of God

—the vision signified that I would come through the personal danger, which I did. Similarly, it showed that the world also would ultimately emerge from the threatening dark cloud of *karma,* but mankind would first have to do its part by turning to God.

The next morning at nine o'clock we started on our trek to the cave. For this part of the journey we had to walk most of the way, but could occasionally ride on horseback or in a *dandi.* This is a little palanquin-like carriage of roughly hewn wood, suspended by rope from two long poles, which are borne on the shoulders of four male porters.

Upward we walked, walked, and walked; sometimes we literally crawled, for in many places the way was very steep. We stopped only briefly at two rest houses along the way. The second one was a government bungalow where we would stay overnight on our return from the cave. Around five in the afternoon, just as the sun was beginning to set over the mountains, we arrived at the cave. The light of the sun, or was it the light of another Power? veiled the whole atmosphere and all objects in a shimmering golden glow.

There are in fact several caves in this area. One is open, hewn by nature out of a giant rock, perhaps the same rocky ledge on which Babaji was standing when Lahiri Mahasaya first saw him. Then there is another cave; to enter it, you must crawl on your hands and knees. This is purportedly the one in which Babaji stayed. Its physical structure, especially the entranceway, has been altered by natural forces during the passage of more than a century since it was occupied by Babaji. In the inner room of this cave we sat for a long time in deep meditation, and prayed for all devotees of our Gurus, and for all mankind. Never before has stillness said so much. The voice of silence spoke loudly of the presence of the Divine. Waves of realization poured through my consciousness; and the prayers I offered that day have since been answered.

As a memento of our visit, and a symbol of the reverence and devotion held by all of Gurudeva's *chelas* for the divine Mahavatar, we left in the cave a small scarf on which the Self-Realization emblem* had been sewn.

After dark, we started our homeward trek. Many villagers had joined our pilgrimage, and a few had thoughtfully and wisely carried along some kerosene lanterns. Voices were raised in songs to God as we wended our way down the mountain. About nine o'clock, we arrived at the humble home of one of the officials of this area, who had accompanied us to the cave; here we were invited to rest. We sat around a blazing fire outside the dwelling, and were served roasted potatoes, black bread, and tea. The bread is baked in ashes, and is as black as can be. I'll never forget how good that meal tasted, in the crisp night air of the holy Himalayas.

It was midnight when we reached the government rest house where we had stopped en route to the cave. Here we were to spend the night—what was left of it! Many people remarked to us afterward that sheer faith brought us through that area at night. It is infested with dangerous snakes, tigers, and leopards. No one would dream of being out there after dark. But it is said that

* See title page. The elements of the insignia depict the spiritual eye of intuition (in the forehead, between the eyebrows), through which man may behold God. The outer border shows a lotus with petals open, ancient symbol of divine awakening.

ignorance is bliss, and it did not occur to us to be frightened. Even if we had known of the dangers, I am sure we would have felt secure. But I wouldn't generally recommend that this journey be made at nighttime!

Throughout the whole day, the experience I had had with Babaji at Katgodam was part of my consciousness; there was also the constant feeling that I was reliving scenes from the past.

"My Nature Is Love"

That night I couldn't sleep. As I sat in meditation, the whole room was lit suddenly with a golden light. The light became a brilliant blue, and there again was the presence of our beloved Babaji! This time he said: "My child, know this: it is not necessary for devotees to come to this spot to find me. Whoever goes within with deep devotion, calling and believing in me, will find my response." This was his message to you all. How true it is. If you only believe, if you just have devotion and silently call on Babaji, you will feel his response.

Then I said, "Babaji, my Lord, our Guru taught us that whenever we want to feel wisdom, we should pray to Sri Yukteswarji, because he is all *jnana,* all wisdom; and whenever we want to feel *ananda* or bliss, we should commune with Lahiri Mahasaya. What is your nature?" As I said it, oh, I felt as though my heart was going to burst with love, such love—a thousand million loves rolled into one! He is all love; his whole nature is *prem* (divine love).

Though unvoiced, a more eloquent response I could not conceive; yet Babaji made it even sweeter and more meaningful as he added these words: "My nature is love; for it is love alone that can change this world."

The presence of the great *avatar* slowly vanished in the diminishing blue light, leaving me joyously enwrapped in love divine.

I remembered what Gurudeva had said to me a short time before he left his body. I had asked him, "Master, usually when the leader goes, an organization no longer grows but begins to die out. How will we carry on without you? What will hold and inspire us when you are no longer here in the flesh?" Never will I forget his answer: "When I have left this world, only love can take my place. Be so drunk with the love of God night and day that you will know nothing else. And give that love to all." This is also Babaji's message—the message for this age.

Love for God, and for God in all, is an eternal summons that has been preached by all the spiritual giants who have graced this earth. It is a truth we must apply in our own lives. It is so essential at this time, when mankind is uncertain of tomorrow, when it seems that hate, selfishness, greed, could destroy the world. We must be divine warriors armed with love, compassion, and understanding; this is what is so vitally needed.

So, my dear ones, I have shared this experience with you so you might know that Babaji lives. He does exist, and his message is an eternal one of divine love. I am not referring to the selfish, narrow, personal, possessive love of ordinary human relationships. I mean the love that Christ gives to his disciples, that Gurudeva gives to us: unconditional divine love. This is the love *we* must give to all. We all cry for it. There is not one of us in this room who doesn't long for love, for a little kindness and understanding.

We are the soul, and the nature of the soul is perfection; so we can never be fully satisfied with anything that is less than perfect. But we can never know what perfection is until we know Him, the Perfect Love, the Father, Mother, Friend, and Beloved: our God.

The Spirit of Truth

Self-Realization Fellowship international headquarters, Los Angeles, California, May 2, 1963

In all my years in the ashrams of Paramahansa Yogananda, I cannot remember many occasions when he delved deeply into metaphysical questions in talking with the resident disciples. It was not because of lack of interest on our part; nor because of any lack of knowledge on his. He purposely refrained from such discussions in order to steer us away from intellectualizing. He did not want us to become preoccupied with philosophical speculations, lest we cease to feel first and foremost a burning interest in knowing, in experiencing, God.

Similarly, we could discuss this evening the question of whether souls are being created continually, and if so, how many new souls God created today, and so on; Guruji occasionally touched on subjects of this kind in his writings. But he didn't consider them of paramount importance, because understanding of such matters comes to all as their Self-unfoldment progresses. Until that direct realization is attained, one who is seeking God should guard against becoming sidetracked and lost in philosophy. One may become very learned in Paramahansaji's teachings, and yet fail to absorb his spirit. I am dedicated to the ideal that the spirit of God and Guru must be manifest in the lives of devotees on this path. Such disciples are the future of this work, because those who assimilate that spirit, through attunement with Guru in meditation, will attain their own Self-realization and all truth to be known. Study Guruji's teachings deeply, yes; but put first things first. Your supreme interest and endeavor should be to experience in your soul the God about whom Gurudeva is teaching you.

I would far rather sit at the feet of one who is drunk with the love of God, and hear him speak of his personal communion with God, than listen to the most brilliant exposition of theoretical philosophy. You would feel empty and restless if we filled our time in the ashram with dry discussion of theories about what God is and does. But when someone talks a little about Him from experience, and you meditate together and feel His presence, you are inwardly satisfied, and you grow spiritually.

Remember these words: So long as there is a desire for anything less than God, one is still struggling with delusion. If Paramahansaji noticed that someone in the ashram was beginning to desire something in preference to God, he would put every possible obstacle in that disciple's path to waken him from his delusion. And if a disciple tried to impress Paramahansaji with remarkable questions, Gurudeva would simply ignore him. But when Paramahansaji felt from a devotee the magnetic pull of sincere longing to know God, he would spend hours with that individual. He would not just talk of spiritual truths, but would guide and encourage in meditation; and he would discipline that devotee—with sharp words if necessary. He trained in that way because his duty as the guru was to help the disciple to recognize and overcome delusion; his mission was not merely to increase man's intellectual knowledge about God, but to lead souls to Him.

Truth Is Fully Understood Only When Experienced

When one perceives any truth deeply, when one loves greatly, he cannot talk easily about his feelings. So it is very difficult for a devotee to put into words a beautiful experience with God. It is so divine, so perfect in itself, that he does not want to speak about it. The saints say that the moment a divine experience is described in words, it becomes cloaked to some degree with imperfection. Words are an imperfect medium, and therefore cannot fully convey perfection. And so it is with Truth. The moment Truth, or God, is merely talked about and not experienced, something is lost. The teachings of Jesus Christ are an example. They are correctly interpreted only when a St. Francis of Assisi, or some other great lover of Christ, is born. And such a devotee is concerned not so much with the words as with the spirit behind them; his desire is to live in the spirit of Christ. That spirit of truth is what Paramahansa Yogananda tried to convey to those who came to him for training.

Most people do not actively seek God because they do not realize that true happiness is not to be found elsewhere. Human craving for fame and power, desire for material plenty, and longing for the recognition of others, all stem from the natural urge of the soul to express its infinite potential. The soul knows its own perfect nature—divinely glorious and all-powerful. But in the deluded ego state we do not know this soul perfection; we are only aware of, and misinterpret, its promptings to manifest our native power and glory.

The Right Way to Satisfy Desires

It is not wrong to have worthy goals and desires; the error lies in trying to express and to satisfy them in finite ways, for then we end up wallowing in delusion. When such desires come, inwardly pray: "Lord, I know that the basis of these longings is the desire of the soul to express its infinite nature, made in Thine image. Help me to satisfy my craving for love, power, and recognition by knowing myself as the soul." This is a wonderful way to reason, using discrimination to overcome delusion.

"But seek ye first the kingdom of God, and His righteousness; and all these things shall be added unto you." I know this to be so. Many years ago, as a young devotee on the path, I realized that in these words Christ voiced the great promise of God that if we first seek the Lord, and if we seek Him above all things, then whatever else we have ever craved will come to us. I determined that I would either prove or disprove this statement in my own life. Whenever moments of doubt came I would renew my inner vow: to use the opportunities in this incarnation to prove whether these words from the Bible are false or true.

The easiest way to follow the spiritual path is to take a principle of philosophy, or a statement of truth, and strive to build your life around it. For each of you there is some particular truth in the scriptures, or in the words of great saints, that you especially cherish because of the inspiration it gives you. Don't be content merely to be inspired by the words. Try every day to the best of your ability to live that truth, so that your inspiration deepens into direct perception.

What most interested Master was the spirit of the devotee—the loving desire and determination to experience God. This is what keeps true spiritual teachings alive and pure. Not all the intellectual learning in the world can do it, because intellectuality too often is a stumbling block between understanding gained from reading or hearing about God, and direct perception of Him. When a seeker personally experiences the love and wisdom of God, no one can shake his conviction. "He who knows, he knows; naught else knows."* That devotee wants only to live Truth, to feel God's presence, and to become one with Him. He has no other ambition or desire.

So, finding God, or even sincerely seeking Him, means the end of all desires, because the relationship with God is all-satisfying. The man of God, being totally fulfilled, has no wish to express himself as an ego-entity separate from God. He is interested only in doing the will of God—sharing Him with others, arousing within them interest not in himself but in God. His greatest joy is to draw others to the one Beloved he adores.

Those who meditate deeply, who practice *Kriya Yoga* faithfully, and who attain direct experience of God, will be the power that will sustain Self-Realization Fellowship. The blueprint for this work was set in the ether by God; it was founded at His behest,† and His

* From *Cosmic Chants,* by Paramahansa Yogananda.

† Paramahansa Yogananda has described in *Autobiography of a Yogi* the singular events leading up to the founding of Self-Realization Fellowship (Yogoda Satsanga Society of India) for the dissemination of *Kriya Yoga* to the world.

love and His will sustain and guide it. I know this beyond doubt. The practice of *Kriya* will bring its own proof of Truth to every generation of disciples of Paramahansa Yogananda.

Do Avatars Have Karma?

Self-Realization Fellowship international headquarters, Los Angeles, California, August 17, 1965

During the talk Sri Daya Mata responded to the following questions: Is the suffering of liberated beings the result of bad *karma* from the past? Does any *karma* result from their actions in this life?

The cumulative results of our right or wrong actions are referred to as our *karma.* The law of *karma* (action) is the law of cause and effect: what we sow we must reap. Good actions bring good results into our lives, bad actions bring negative results and suffering. All mankind is subject to this law, except those rare souls who have attained aboveness by realizing their oneness with God. Souls such as Jesus and Krishna do suffer on earth, but to say that their suffering is the result of any wrong deeds of their own is to carry logic to a ridiculous conclusion. Following this line of reasoning we would have to assume that the Lord has very bad *karma* for having created suffering mankind. And if we are individualized sparks of God, as the scriptures teach, then our suffering must be the result of His wrong actions, and so it is He who is suffering through us. But it is illogical to think that the law of *karma* can be applied to God, or to those who have become one with God and have thus gone beyond the reach of His laws. The snake carries poison in its fangs, but it never dies from its own venom. The Infinite carries the law of duality, the poison of *maya,* within Himself, but He is unaffected by it. He who is one with God similarly remains untouched by *maya*. Only those who are subject to that law of duality suffer from its poison. Even great saints may have some vestiges of *karma* to be worked out. But when a soul has been liberated and then returns to earth he is free of karmic imperatives. No matter what he does, he is in full control of himself and the results of his actions.

A Master Can Be Fiery Without Anger

For example, it would not be correct to say that Gurudeva Paramahansa Yogananda was capable of anger; I never found him angry, but he could be fiery when necessary. If one has mastery of an instrument, he can use it effectively according to its intended purpose. If he has no control over that instrument, he can misuse it. God gave man the power to speak and act with fire. Even Christ showed that; he was fiery when he drove the money-changers from the temple.* He did not meekly approach them and say: "Now this is a naughty thing you are doing, my children, please take your business transactions out of here." He overthrew their tables and set loose the doves that were being sold. Similarly, all masters—those who are master of themselves—can display a seemingly wrathful disposition at times, but they are in full control of it. Any ordinary person who is prone to anger and has no control over it must learn to conquer his emotion or suffer the karmic consequences.

* Matthew 21:12.

Paramahansaji said that when he was a young boy he once became angry at a bully who used to pick on the smaller boys. He beat that bully in a fight and then vowed he would never get angry again. Even this anger has to be qualified. When a great soul is born in this world, he first expresses through the body and mentality of a child; he has some of the limitations of a child. But hidden within him, as the flower is hidden within the seed, is the essential divinity of his nature; the pattern of greatness is there. So Gurudeva had a child's anger; but even that was governed by a subconscious wisdom, for it was spurred by a righteous cause.

The fact that Paramahansaji was conscious in his mother's womb shows that he was no ordinary child. He had attained oneness with God many incarnations ago. He came in this life as a master. But he was so humble, he didn't say much about himself before the public. He never declared his greatness. That is the way of the truly great. Having perfect humility, they never think of their own eminence. The Divine is also that way. He never speaks of His incomparable greatness even to His saints. But we can behold it when we look at nature. See His beautiful form and intelligence therein: power in the ocean, magnificence in the mountains, omniscience in the laws that govern the universe—in these we find His unspoken sublimity.

In the same way real nobleness in people is unspoken by them. It is so with all great ones; it was so with Gurudeva.

As Actors Play a Role, Avatars Take On Name and Form

To appear on earth in human form, however, even a master has to take on a certain amount of delusion or the very atoms of his body would not hold together; but that is not *karma*. The delusion essential for a manifested form is what Jesus alluded to when he had just come out of the tomb after his crucifixion and said to Mary Magdalene, "Touch me not; for I am not yet ascended to my Father."* When any soul, even a Christ, descends into the world of duality and takes on a human form, he thereby accepts certain limitations. But taking on the compulsions of the law of *karma* is not one of them. He still remains above and beyond all *karma*.

In the spiritual lore of India, there are countless stories, true and mythological, the purpose of which is to illustrate—and thus simplify—profound metaphysical truths. As an example, there is a story told about Lord Krishna: It is said that he was walking with one of his devotees through the fields of a little village in India and noticed a sow suckling her piglets. The mother pig was grunting now and then, talking to her babies, and they were squeaking contentedly. Lord Krishna saw in this a beautiful expression of motherly love. He said to his disciple, "I'm going to enter the body of that sow and have that experience for a while." Krishna's form disappeared, losing its identity in the mother pig.

Now most people don't feel very attracted to pigs. But when I was young, we used to visit my grandmother's farm every summer, and I thought there was nothing cuter or sweeter than the little pink piglets. They were adorable, and so clean and affectionate. We used to carry them to the lawn in front of the house and play with them by the hour. So when I first heard this story I could understand and appreciate Lord Krishna's feeling.

* John 20:17.

Months went by and the disciple began to worry about Lord Krishna and why he had not yet returned. The devotee went back to the field where he had left Krishna. He saw the mother pig, happily surrounded by her piglets. "Krishna, my Lord, what are you doing? You said you were going to come out of that form after a while."

Krishna answered, "Oh! this is such a sweet experience, I don't want to leave."

"My Lord, you are Krishna! You can't remain bound like this! Come out!"

Krishna consented. "You are right. Take a spear and drive it into this form." When the disciple had obeyed, the form of Krishna emerged from the sow's body, unchanged, untrammeled by that experience.

So, in the same way, Christ and the masters have no *karma,* nor are they affected more than momentarily and superficially by their assumed limitations. Only when they incarnate do they temporarily limit themselves by that bodily encasement. God has no form; He is not an old man with a white beard sitting on a throne someplace in heaven. He is Spirit, unlimited, unconfined. When He temporarily assumes a form, it is only the form that is limited.

Since the great ones come on earth only to play a role, there is no *karma* for them. Jesus Christ was bound for a time by his form, and with the coming of his crucifixion he knew the role he was destined to play according to the will of the Infinite: to demonstrate the immortality of the soul. Thus he said, "Destroy this temple, and in three days I will raise it up."* He had

* John 2:19.

that power. But it would be false to say that Christ did not suffer. Of course he suffered! He was in that body and he experienced real pain when they scourged him and pierced his flesh with the nails, the wreath of thorns, and the spear. He knew what pain was, or he would not have cried: "My God, my God, why hast Thou forsaken me?"* But in the next instant he conquered the delusion of that limitation. This gives hope to us all, that we too can conquer if we keep on trying.

Our Real Strength Comes from Self-Surrender

There is a saying that what we cannot cure we must endure. We should acquire a bit more endurance in this world. Let us not be so weak, whining and crying and feeling that life is hopeless. So long as there is life there is hope. We should never, never inwardly give up. Rather, we should mentally throw ourselves at the feet of Him who is our strength, our power, our love, and our joy. Real strength comes from such self-surrender. It is hard to do; if it were easy, everyone would do it. But it is very difficult to give up this little self. To learn that lesson is why we are here on this earth.

As with Christ, so with all great souls. After they have completed their role on earth they must again rid themselves of all consciousness of form. At the approach of death, even with the greatest, there is a sudden shock. When the message came to Lahiri Mahasaya from Babaji: "Tell Lahiri that the stored-up power for this life runs low; it is nearly finished,"† Lahiri Mahasaya shuddered. Similarly with Swami Sri Yukteswar when his time came to leave the body. Such is the

* Matthew 27:46.

† *Autobiography of a Yogi,* chapter 36.

power of delusion. This momentary fear does not minimize the greatness of divine souls.

Sooner or Later God Fulfills All Desires

As liberated souls are not bound by *karma,* neither are they bound by their desires. When Lahiri Mahasaya received *Kriya Yoga* initiation, Babaji created for him a golden palace to satisfy his *chela's* long-forgotten desire from the past.* Yet Lahiri Mahasaya was an *avatar,* and such desires no longer bound him. The Indian sages say that it takes eight million lives to evolve to this human form, and we have already passed countless incarnations in human form. Through all those lives we have had millions, perhaps trillions, of desires, some of them for little things, like ice cream. When one at last finds God, everything he has ever craved, even the slightest desire, will be ferreted out and satisfied sometime by the Infinite. Yet one supposedly gives up all other desires for the sake of finding God. This is renunciation? You give up nothing! You renounce only *the time* when fulfillment is going to come to you. Because so long as there is even the slightest yearning in you for anything, that desire must find fulfillment, whether by being washed away, or neutralized, or satisfied. Renunciation simply means that you say: "O Lord, I want only You! Now You worry about me. This soul, this 'I,' belongs to You—now it is Your problem. I have no greater desire than for You alone."

Far back in one of Lahiri Mahasaya's past lives there must have been a desire for a palace. It was not something that was holding him back from spiritual attainment, for that attainment had already come to

* See *Autobiography of a Yogi,* chapter 34.

him, neutralizing past desires. It is as if you came to me and told me that as a child you always loved ice cream, and, to please you, I arrange to give you ice cream. You do not need it, because you have long since outgrown the yearning for it. I understand that it is not, and never was, a condition of your life without which you simply could not go on.

For instance, after each of Gurudeva's lectures in Salt Lake City (before I came here to the Mount Washington headquarters) I had the privilege of accompanying his assistants to his sitting room in the hotel. He would relax and talk informally to us about his classes or other spiritual subjects. And always before I left for home, he ordered ice cream with chocolate sauce. I had once said to him that I loved ice cream with chocolate sauce on it! So throughout the three months he was in Salt Lake City we had ice cream with chocolate sauce every night.

About ten years later Gurudeva went back there and I was in his party. We all stayed in the same hotel where he had lectured before. That first evening we gathered in his sitting room, and found he had ordered ice cream with chocolate sauce. He looked at me with a twinkle, as though to say: "This is for you." He knew that fulfillment of that desire was no longer essential; it was just an expression of affection—giving what had once meant so much to me.

Similarly, the creation of a palace was Babaji's way of saying to Lahiri Mahasaya, "Since you once long ago had a craving for a palace, I wish to give it to you." It was in no way a condition that had to be fulfilled before Lahiri Mahasaya could attain liberation. He had already attained that. What would a palace mean to someone in that state of consciousness? In my consciousness it means nothing; how could it mean anything to someone of Lahiri Mahasaya's stature?

Truth is so interesting, so fascinating! One can go on discussing it endlessly. But in the ultimate analysis, the highest truth is to learn to be in love with the One. In that love we find oneness with the Infinite Being. Then there are no more desires, limitations, or queries. That is why Gurudeva taught us that above all else we must be in love with God.

Our Oneness in God

Condensation of talk on opening night of Self-Realization Fellowship 1975 Convocation, Los Angeles, California, July 25, 1975

How nice it is to see so many devotees gathered here from all parts of the world on this very special day.* These convocations are held every five years, and many of you were here on the occasion of our Golden Anniversary Convocation in 1970. Now we honor the fifty-fifth year of the founding of Gurudeva Paramahansa Yogananda's work here in the West.

These next ten days will be filled with much activity; and of course our heartfelt wish, our prayer, is that they may be filled with great inspiration for all of you. The search for God, as you know, is an individual pursuit. No one else can give us God, any more than someone else can drink water for us when we are thirsting. Guruji used to say that if you are thirsty, just reading about water or hearing eloquent sermons about it will not satisfy you. It is only when you go to the well and drink deep of its cool, refreshing water that your thirst is completely satisfied. So in the same way we can

* July 25 is celebrated by Self-Realization Fellowship/Yogoda Satsanga Society of India as Mahavatar Babaji Commemoration Day, the anniversary of Paramahansa Yogananda's meeting the Mahavatar. This unusual event, and much more about the life of Babaji, was recorded by Paramahansa Yogananda in *Autobiography of a Yogi*.

speak through endless aeons about God, we can read countless sermons about God, but they will never be able to quench the inner drought of our souls. Only one thing can satisfy our yearning, can fulfill our need, and that is to experience the love of God. So we begin the Convocation with that thought as our supreme goal.

This day is the day set aside annually by Self-Realization Fellowship to honor Mahavatar Babaji. Therefore it is fitting on this occasion to speak of his mission in the world. It was he who chose Guruji, many, many years ago in India, and sent him to the West with a message as old as the ages, yet still vibrantly new and stirring today in its import for mankind. Truth is eternal. It isn't the possession of any one era, group of people, nationality, or religious body; it belongs to all mankind. It is truth eternal—nurtured in India—that Babaji intended be spread throughout the world when he wisely chose for the task his beloved Yogananda, whose life so purely reflected divinity. Thus Paramahansa Yogananda brought to us these great teachings of Self-Realization, and Babaji's unique gift to the world, *Kriya Yoga*. Paramahansaji's appeal to mankind is: "My children, there is a God. You have read your various scriptures in all the world religions, wherein are recorded the divine experiences of God-realization. But this isn't enough. You must make truth your own, and *Kriya* is the way."

It was in India that techniques of concentration and meditation for realizing God were first discovered. And now, as Guruji predicted back in 1934, India's science of meditation is sweeping the Western world.

There is a story told in India which illustrates that no one has a monopoly on truth. Six boys, blind since birth, were washing their father's elephant. One was washing the tail; he concluded that the elephant was like a rope. Another was washing the legs; he described the elephant as being like four pillars. The third son said, "You are both wrong. The elephant is like two fans that swing back and forth." He had been washing the ears. Another said, "No! the elephant is like a vast wall." He had been washing the animal's sides. The fifth son had been washing the elephant's tusks. He was convinced that the elephant was just a couple of bones. Finally, the last of the blind boys said, "I must tell you that all of you are wrong. The elephant is like a heavy snake." He had been washing the trunk.

The argument continued, each boy sure that he knew the truth as to what the elephant was like. The father saw his children fighting and asked them what the trouble was. They explained, and appealed to him, "Which of us is right?" The father answered, "Well, my dear sons, you are all right, and you are all wrong as well! You see, the elephant is like not one, but all these various things you have described. You have not taken into consideration that each one is only a part of the whole elephant."

It is the same with truth. No religion has a monopoly on truth; all contain something of the eternal verity. When we go beyond the barriers of sectarian beliefs and sit quietly in meditation, churning the ether with our thought, "My God, my God, my God, reveal Thyself, reveal Thyself," and silently plunge deeper and deeper into the well of inspiration and truth hidden within the soul, we begin to perceive what God is. Then we spontaneously honor Him in all religions, and feel respect for every sincere teacher. We know our God to be the God of all mankind and that the multifarious expressions of truth are a part of the whole. Through this realization we come also to a deeper understanding of our fellowman.

The Brotherhood of Man, the Fatherhood of God

Let me read something prophetic that Gurudeva said, in this very hall,* in 1937: "It is a new world we face. . . . and we must mold ourselves to the changes. An absolute necessity for the new generation is the recognition of the divinity of all mankind, and the sweeping away of all divisive barriers. I cannot conceive of a Jesus Christ, or a Lord Krishna, or the *rishis* of old calling any man a Christian, a Hindu, a Jew, and so forth. I *can* conceive of their calling every man 'my brother.' There will be no new order built on contempt of other races or on a 'chosen people' complex; but rather on recognition of the divinity of every man who walks the face of this earth, and on recognition of the common fatherhood of God."

Guruji used to say that if Jesus Christ, Bhagavan Krishna, Lord Buddha, and all the others who have communed with God were gathered together, there would be no quarreling among them, because they drink from the same fountain of Truth. They are one in God. He is manifest in them all. It is the misdirected enthusiasm of small-minded disciples that causes division. We must do away with narrow-mindedness if we

* The auditorium of the United Methodist Church in downtown Los Angeles. Paramahansa Yogananda spoke here at a conference of religious leaders on February 25, 1937. For its 1975 Convocation, Self-Realization Fellowship reserved this spacious auditorium for a number of special activities.

would be true disciples of the great ones. We should honor all religions; and we should love all people, be they black, yellow, red, white, or brown. It is nonsense to judge a man by his color. Electricity may flow into a red bulb, a green bulb, a yellow bulb, or a blue bulb; but would you say that the electricity is different in each one? No. Similarly, God shines equally in all human bulbs as the immortal soul. The color of the skin makes no difference. We must do away with narrow prejudices. God wants us to take the best of the ideals and qualities of all peoples and make them our own.

Where Two or Three Are Gathered Together

In closing, let me share with you some thoughts of Gurudeva's: "We must establish meditation groups and centers all over the world. But hives of temples and centers that are empty of the honey of God-realization do not interest me; the hive of organization must be filled with the honey of God's presence."

Meditating together is the way to fill the organizational hive with God's honey. When I first came to the ashram, Gurudeva said to me, "Gather two or three around you and meditate." It is what his guru used to tell him also. Now, as Gurudeva wished, I see that you devotees from all parts of the world do gather in small groups, not for discussing philosophy or for personal ambition to be teachers, but to seek God in meditation. When even a few of you meditate together, each one strengthens the others in their desire for God.

Gurudeva said: "The masters of India say that the purpose of religion is not to create certain doctrines to be followed blindly, but to show mankind the perennial method of finding everlasting happiness. As the businessman tries to alleviate the suffering of others by supplying some need; as every man is an agent of God for doing some good on earth, so Christ, Krishna, Buddha—all the great ones—came on earth to bestow on mankind the highest good: knowledge of the path to Eternal Bliss, and the example of their sublime lives to inspire us to follow it. Someday you will have to leave the body. No matter how powerful you are, the body will eventually have to be buried beneath the sod. There is no time to be wasted. The Yoga methods taught by my beloved Christ and Krishna do destroy ignorance and suffering by enabling man to attain his own Self-realization and union with God."*

[Daya Mataji asks God's blessings on the assemblage, speaking in the languages of some of the twenty-eight countries represented, and concludes with the following words:]

Divine Mother didn't bless me with the ability to be a linguist! But I speak to you in the universal language of my soul: I give to all of you my soul's divine love and friendship. That love which I feel for my beloved God, I feel for each one of you who are my own—you who are traveling toward the one supreme goal: God alone. God bless you.

* From "Christ and Krishna: Avatars of One Truth," in *Man's Eternal Quest*, by Paramahansa Yogananda.

The Only Answer to Life

Indo-American Spiritual Ensemble,
sponsored by the Government of India Cultural Center,
San Francisco, California, March 23, 1975

It is a pleasure to come here this evening as a part of the great purpose for which this meeting has been called: the integration of religious thought.

At the turn of the century, a great spiritual giant came to America: Swami Vivekananda. He introduced for the first time here the immortal message of the eternal religion of India, sowing the seeds of *Sanatan Dharma.* Some decades later, another enlightened teacher, Paramahansa Yogananda, was sent by his guru to speak at the Congress of Religious Liberals in Boston; he, too, sowed the seeds of India's immortal religion.*

At the age of seventeen I was privileged to begin my study at the feet of Paramahansa Yogananda, receiving his discipline, and recording his words. In 1934 he stated publicly, "There will come a day, after I have left this physical form, when there will be a great surge of spiritual enthusiasm and interest in God. The message of India, the spiritual leader of the world, will sweep

* Paramahansa Yogananda was the first missionary of India's religion to remain in this country and teach for a long period, more than thirty years.

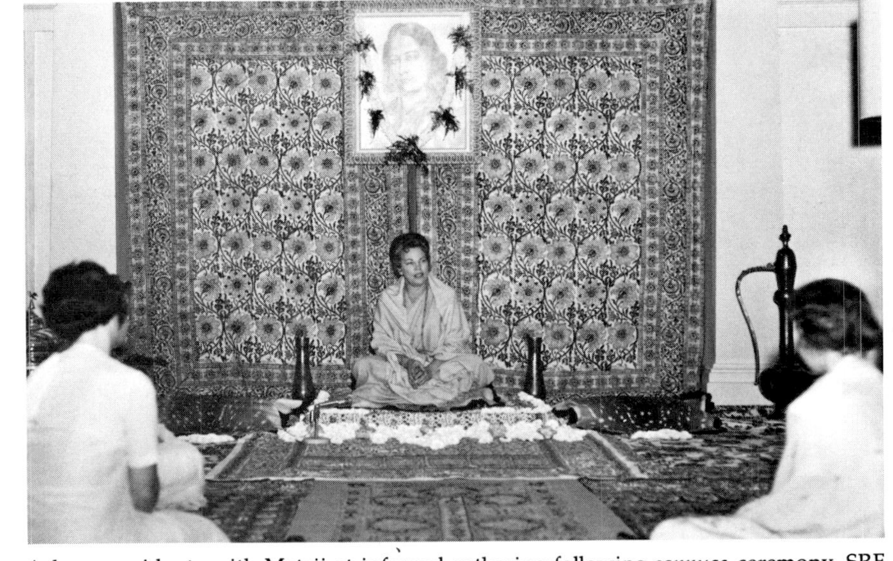

Ashram residents with Mataji at informal gathering following *sannyas* ceremony, SRF international headquarters, Los Angeles, 1965

"In every phase of our lives—in our work, meditation, struggling with difficulties, enjoying simple pleasures—we must continually be anchored inwardly in the thought: 'God! God! God!'"

In the village of Palpara, West Bengal, India, 1973

"Boundaries disappear in united love for God as the Father of all. He must be the one common ideal, the

Celebration of Holi, Ranchi, March 1973; festive spiritual holiday. *Above:* Teachers and students of YSS schools receive shower of colored powder from hand of Mataji. *Below:* A child, intent on his observance, places colored powder at Mataji's feet.

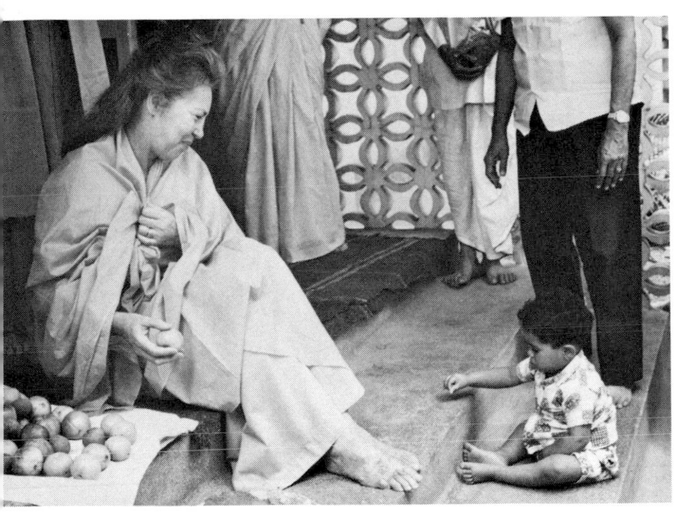

"When you look inward to God you see utter simplicity, divine and joyous simplicity. That's the way God is."

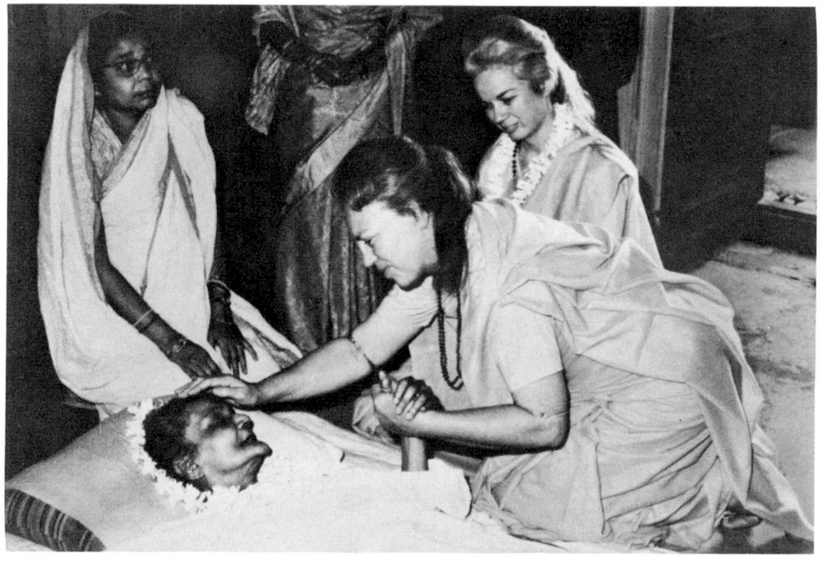

Calcutta, 1968

"We should realize that we are not alone, that we never have been and never will be alone. From the very beginning of time, God has been with us, and throughout eternity He will be with us."

the earth." These words have rung in my ears many times, because I see this is what has happened today. We find that more than ever there is a yearning for togetherness, and a yearning to find the answers to all of those questions that plague man, regardless of the color of his skin, or of the part of this earth in which he was born.

We have come to a new age, wherein it becomes necessary for mankind to unite. No wars will save humanity. We can hearken back to the words of Christ two thousand years ago: "If you use the sword, you will fall by the sword."* How bitterly we have paid in this modern day. We are facing now what seems to be an unknown future.

There is chaos amongst the young people of all countries. In my travels two years ago through European countries, and then up into Afghanistan, I noted how the young people were on the move. They were seeking and confused, discontented with what they had received from life, and with the examples that had been set before them. There is discontentment in communities, discontentment in nations, discontentment throughout the whole world.

There is only one answer to life and the purpose of man's being. If it is true that man is made in the image of God—as every religious prophet has taught—then it follows that this image lies within every one of us. It is for us to strive to the best of our ability to manifest that goodness and purity, that magnificence which lies within the human breast.

* "Then said Jesus unto him, Put up again thy sword into his place: for all they that take the sword shall perish with the sword" (Matthew 26:52).

The Bhagavad Gita, along with the Christian scripture, tells us that the purpose of man is to know God, to love God, and to serve God through mankind. This message, being immortal truth, is as important today as when uttered millenniums ago by the great spiritual giants.

If we scan our inner self, we will find that we have come to that point in our lives wherein we feel a hunger, a yearning, a need for a kind of love that will consume us with total fulfillment; and for a complete security that nothing in this world can give—neither money nor health, nor any amount of intellectual understanding. This, then, brings us to the Gita's message, which is that meditation plus right activity is the way to truth, the way back to God, the Source of what we seek.

In all religions, though the method may be called by various names, the follower is taught to practice spiritual silence, or meditation. Christianity teaches: "Pray unceasingly."* Today, more than at any other time that we can recall, you will find in colleges, in the United Nations, in many important establishments, a little quiet place where one can go and sit quietly to talk to his God in the language of his heart. This communion is being practiced by millions of earnest souls.

We were put on earth that we might learn to know the One from whom we have all come. We are His children. Isn't it a strange thing that we utilize everything He has given us, and yet forget the very One who has traveled with us through countless incarnations past, and who will be with us through those yet to come?

* I Thessalonians 5:17: "Pray without ceasing."

Intelligence, love, freedom of will, everything that we express in our daily lives, comes from only one Power, God alone. We cut short our memory of God while utilizing all of the endowments that have come from Him.

What is "right activity" as spoken of in the Gita? It means to adhere — in thought, first, then in speech and action—to those principles that bring forth good. Strive for truthfulness; all religions teach this. Strive for brotherhood; all teach this. Honesty, purity, high moral principles—no religion teaches otherwise. But these mankind has largely forgotten. This is the reason for the terrible chaos we find ourselves in today.

My duties require me to travel around the world periodically. In my journeys, I find more and more that souls such as all of you gathered here, and young people especially, are taking a deep interest in knowing what life is, what truth is, and, above all, in embracing the eternal religion, *Sanatan Dharma,* of India. That "religion" appealed to me many years ago as a young seeker, because I had the notion that it wasn't enough to hear magnificent discourses about God, nor to read about God. I used to look at the various teachers I visited and think, "Yes, but do you love God? I am seeking someone who can instill in me the kind of love that will so inflame my soul that I will know nothing but my God, and devote myself to serving Him, and through Him, to serving my brothers in all parts of the world." I found that someone in a great son of India, my gurudeva, Paramahansa Yogananda.

It is a blessed privilege to join with souls like you in speaking of this immortal religion of India. I should like, in these words written by Paramahansaji, to sum up what life is all about, and how we, as God's children, can come to know Him and to have a sweeter, more intimate relationship with Him.

[Daya Mata closed her talk with a poem by Paramahansa Yogananda.]

GOD! GOD! GOD!

From the depths of slumber,
As I ascend the spiral stairway of wakefulness,
I whisper:
God! God! God!

Thou art the food, and when I break my fast
Of nightly separation from Thee,
I taste Thee, and mentally say:
God! God! God!

No matter where I go, the spotlight of my mind
Ever keeps turning on Thee;
And in the battle din of activity my silent war-cry is ever:
God! God! God!

When boisterous storms of trials shriek
And worries howl at me,
I drown their noises, loudly chanting:
God! God! God!

When my mind weaves dreams
With threads of memories,
On that magic cloth I do emboss:
God! God! God!

Every night, in time of deepest sleep,
My peace dreams and calls: Joy! Joy! Joy!
And my joy comes singing evermore:
God! God! God!

In waking, eating, working, dreaming, sleeping,
Serving, meditating, chanting, divinely loving,
My soul constantly hums, unheard by any:
God! God! God!

God bless you all.

Walk Inwardly with God

Self-Realization Fellowship international headquarters, Los Angeles, California, February 9, 1956

Our attention should be so riveted on the Divine Mother that we are not inwardly affected by changing circumstances in our outer life: sorrow and disappointment should not much move us, nor should material pleasures unduly attract us. I remember someone's saying to Paramahansaji, "Well, a state like that would surely be most dull and uninteresting." Master answered, "On the contrary, when one is absorbed in the Divine Bliss, in the consciousness and awareness of the Divine Mother's presence, one enjoys the good things of this earth with greater appreciation, but without the attachment and sorrow that usually result from engaging in worldly activities."

We should learn to be neither attached to pleasure nor fearful of pain. We should accept what life gives without being too much elated or too much discouraged. This is the state of the truly spiritual man. It isn't some great strength that we can gather suddenly when we need it to face a big problem. This consciousness has to be built up gradually within us, by training ourselves to react properly to everyday problems and occurrences.

Master lived in that consciousness of Divine Mother wherein nothing external could touch him inwardly. Rajarsi* manifested that state, and so did our blessed Gyanamata.† It should become a part of our everyday life also.

We should learn to walk inwardly with God, free of any attachment to our material nature or to worldly pleasures or conditions. We should banish anger, greed, jealousy, hate, pride, and resentment. To be master of emotions, desires, and human nature is the goal of the spiritual man. Self-mastery is what every human being, consciously or unconsciously, is striving toward; because only as master of himself can man be truly happy. We should make the effort to arrive at that state wherein we are able to keep our composure under all circumstances. That perfect calmness and equanimity cannot be acquired through any means except deep meditation—drawing closer to the Divine Source whence the soul, our real nature, originally sprang. Only by commingling the little droplet of our consciousness with the Divine Ocean in meditation are we able to emulate the example, the ideal blissful state, of the saints.

The personality traits we manifest, aside from those qualities born of our unity with Spirit, are a cloak that we put on—an outer appearance that does not express our true feelings, our true inner nature. We have to take our consciousness deep within and strive to feel our oneness with God. Then when our consciousness returns to the world and to the conduct of outer life, we are able to act in such a way that we reflect the divine nature that we feel, that we truly are, within.

* Rajarsi Janakananda. See page x.

† See page 77 n.

God first, God last, God always—God alone! We must hold to that ideal, to that thought. No matter how many times we slip, if we continue to strive, that ideal will eventually become a part of us. Rather, we become a part of it; we become identified with that goal, it becomes the governing, motivating force blessing and guiding our lives.

Never be discouraged. Never think that you cannot make the spiritual grade, no matter how steep it seems at times. One of the most consoling and heartening encouragements Master gave to us was this reminder: "A saint is a sinner who never gave up." We should remember it whenever we get discouraged, or feel that we have fallen short of our spiritual goal. The saving grace of the would-be saint is that he never gives up, he always keeps on trying, no matter how many times he falls, no matter how many mistakes he makes. By never giving up, we prove to God that our devotion, our loyalty, our desire for Him are unconditional. When the Lord is once convinced that it is He alone we want, that it is to Him alone that we turn, then He is satisfied in spite of all our weakness and shortcomings. Then God takes us by the hand, "and He walks with us and He talks with us, and He tells us we are His own."*

*Paraphrased from the well-known hymn, *In the Garden,* by C. Austin Miles.

Learning to Behave

Compilation

Gurudeva Paramahansa Yogananda used to tell us that his guru, Swami Sri Yukteswar, often gave this advice: "Learn to behave." When Gurudeva first said this to me, I thought: "Oh, that's simple. All I have to do is be polite and kind every day—there's nothing to it!" I had much to learn! There is a lot to it—learning to behave is everything. Attitude of mind is everything.

No devotee ever got very far on the path to God until he began to introspect and gradually rout out all the evil or negative tendencies that kept him conscious of himself as an ego, as a body. "This is mine!" "My feelings are hurt!" "I" this, and "I" that—thinking this way is a great mistake. But the more one meditates the more he realizes that this "I" is not the doer. God is the only Doer. The devotee should pray, "Lord, make me a more willing instrument. Guide this instrument with Thy wisdom, that it may perform the duties Thou dost set before it; that it may serve in whatever way Thou dost wish."

It isn't enough that we abstain from evil actions. It isn't enough that we learn to control our tempers so that in moments of stress we do not say anything unkind. It is not enough merely to silence our tongues while retaining evil and anger in the mind. We must overcome from within. If wrong behavior is worth resisting in action, it is worth resisting in thought also. Desist in both thought and deed.

One Cannot Successfully Entertain Both Good and Evil

At one time or another all devotees who determine to seek God pass through a state wherein they cling to both their good and their bad habits. Such devotees find, upon analyzing their thoughts, that although they are extremely eager to find God, and although they are trying sincerely to establish good habits of meditation and spiritual action, still they feel very, very reluctant to give up their bad habits—anger, moods, likes and dislikes. Yet it is not possible to reconcile the presence of both good and evil actions in a life that is dedicated to God. It will not work. Our minds have to accept the fact, otherwise we will not make a real effort to conquer moods and wrong habits. By meditating more deeply, and by performing all duties with the thought of serving God, the devotee gradually begins to strengthen his good habits and tendencies. As these gain the upper hand, bad habits begin to lose their hold on him.

So in seeking God and in striving to be good we must accept the necessary corollary of giving up evil. One cannot successfully entertain both good and evil within himself. Sooner or later the conflict between them will shatter his peace of mind. I remember Gurudeva's saying many times to devotees: "If you think you can hold on to your anger, your jealousy, your selfish desires, and still find God, you are mistaken. You cannot do it!"

Strive always with utmost effort to overcome unspiritual qualities, but do not be discouraged if it takes a long time. The Lord is not interested in how long it takes us to banish our faults—His chief concern is that in thought and action we *continuously resist* our wrong tendencies. As we make an effort to improve, and to meditate longer and more deeply, we shall find from time to time—often when we least expect it—a burden lifted from our consciousness, leaving us completely free of some bad habit or tendency.

The Transforming Power of a Glimpse of God

Gurudeva used to say to us: "If just once you get a glimpse of Divine Mother, you will forsake all contrary desires and ambitions. You will feel no longing for anything else." This is true; but it doesn't mean that temptation is removed from your path. The devotee faces many temptations, many tests, many trials; but because he has felt the love of God, he is able to discriminate. He wants nothing that will cause him to feel separated from God. If the devotee concentrates too much on material pursuits, he feels God withdrawing from his heart, and so he determines, "I must meditate more." If he is in the habit of criticizing others or of being oversensitive suddenly the thought comes to him, "What am I raising so much fuss about? Why don't I change myself? Why do I waste my time trying to justify to others my beliefs, my opinions, my convictions, when my time could be better spent in the thought of God?"

In Self-Mastery Nothing Can Disturb or Shake Us

Learning to rise above the body, learning to rise above desires, learning to rise above habits, learning to rise above moods—therein lies self-mastery. Whenever anything comes to disturb the mind, know that God is testing you, disciplining you. If that test can "throw" you, if it can take your mind away from God, if it can upset you, if it can rouse your temper, if it can make you feel self-pity, then you have found a weak link in the chain of your consciousness.

A real devotee is one whose mind is always immersed in Divine Mother—Her calmness, Her peace. To achieve this blessed state we should struggle for that mastery of self wherein nothing can disturb or shake us. Take philosophically the trials that come to you each day, and do your best to adjust yourselves. Be like the cork on the ocean; no matter how much the waves toss the cork about, it always rides on the crest. No matter how severely life tosses us about, we should not allow ourselves to sink into the ocean of sadness, the ocean of delusion.

Obstacles Are Meant to Strengthen Us

Realize how far you have yet to go on the path that leads back to God, and how important it is to rise above the trifling troubles that occur in daily life. Ignore the pinpricks of difficulties. They distract your attention from your goal: to find God, to establish your unity with Him, through right action and through manifesting His divine qualities in your life.

The road of life is filled with many rocks of trials and tribulations. We cannot expect God to remove them from our path, but we can ask Him to give us the strength and the wisdom to avoid stumbling over them. God does not intend that we have no obstacles in life, for then we would remain weak. He wants us to become stronger by surmounting them.

To gain this strength, we need follow only one simple formula: increase our love for Divine Mother.

With the expansion of our heart's feeling for God, every mountain of difficulty is reduced to a tiny molehill. Everything that before seemed impossible of accomplishment becomes realizable.

The Greatest Force in the World

Love is the greatest motivating force in the world; and the highest expression of love in creation is the love of God. The more you put your concentration on the love of Divine Mother—even though you can't always feel it in your heart—and the more you pray to Her that you might experience that divine love and that you might give it to others, the more you will gradually feel within you the awakening of that love. There is nothing else like it! The joy of that blissful divine love is the balm for all the ills of mankind.

Never rest—not for a moment, night or day—until you feel God's love in your heart. Once you do, it opens up tremendous understanding. You will realize that God has caused the world to withhold perfect love and understanding and friendship in order that we might receive these things directly from Him. He loves us so much that He doesn't want us to have total fulfillment on the human plane, lest we become satisfied with fragments of temporal joy and become lost to Him forever.

Love God so deeply—with all your heart, with all your mind, and with all your soul—that night and day, no matter what you are doing, the thought of Him is ever in the background of your mind. Gurudeva often used to say, "Watch your thoughts. See how much time you spend in useless, foolish, or negative thoughts; and observe how much time you spend thinking of God."

Never be satisfied until always, regardless of what duties you are performing or what pleasures you are engaged in, the thought of God is present in the back of your mind, the love of God is uppermost in your heart. Even then, do not be content until you attain the ultimate goal of every devotee—the complete divine union with Him that the great ones have experienced.

How to Know God

Compilation

Because we have been made in the image of God, we will never be satisfied until we unite ourselves with Him once again. When we seek perfect love from human beings, we do not find it. Gurudeva Paramahansa Yogananda used to remind us, "Everything will disappoint you except God." This is why it is so important to fill your consciousness with the thought of the Lord.

The worldly man's consciousness dwells principally in the coccygeal, sacral, and lumbar centers of the spine;* he seldom lifts his consciousness above them. Whenever one indulges in moods or temper or any of

* Yoga teaches that within man's brain and spinal plexuses are seven subtle centers of life and consciousness. Yoga treatises refer to these centers as *muladhara* (coccygeal), *svadhisthana* (sacral), *manipura* (lumbar), *anahata* (dorsal), *vishuddha* (cervical), *ajna* (medulla and Christ center between the eyebrows), and *sahasrara* (thousand-petaled lotus in the cerebrum). Without the specialized powers lodged therein, the body would be an inert mass of clay. Man's baser materialistic instincts and motivations have their correlative powers in the lower three subtle spinal centers. The higher centers are the fountainhead of divine feeling and inspiration and spiritual perception. According to the nature of man's thoughts and desires, his consciousness is drawn to and concentrated in the corresponding center of power and activity.

the negative qualities of the human emotional nature, the consciousness is drawn down to the three lower centers in the spine.

The divine man's consciousness stays principally in the dorsal, or heart center, where he feels pure love for God and for all mankind; in the medullary center, where he comprehends all creation as God's holy vibration, hearing it as the cosmic sound of *Aum*;* and in the Christ or *Kutastha* center,† where his consciousness expands, enabling him to experience, through direct perception, his oneness with God in every atom in creation. Whenever we express kindness, forgiveness, understanding, endurance, courage, faith, or love, our consciousness is drawn to these higher cerebrospinal centers.

Self-Analysis, a Good Way to Judge Spiritual Progress

One of the ways by which we may really know if we are progressing spiritually is to analyze ourselves honestly. We may be entertaining certain beliefs about our spiritual qualifications and unfoldment that are not true; we believe the best of ourselves simply because that is what we want to believe. We should examine our thoughts closely. Paramahansaji used to tell us to pause periodically during each day's activities and ask ourselves, "Where is my consciousness?" The answer often brings a rude awakening. If our consciousness isn't engrossed in silent communion with God, in love and concern for our fellowman, in the feeling of expansion that comes with listening inwardly to the sound of

* The "Word" or "voice of many waters" of the Bible. (See John 1:1, Revelation 19:6, Ezekiel 43:2.)

† At the point between the eyebrows.

Aum, then we must admit that we still have a long way to go on the spiritual path.

Meditation Transforms Our Life

The first step is meditation. It is the most important, for only if we are meditating deeply and regularly may we know for certain that we are arriving at the divine state that otherwise we oftentimes just delude ourselves into thinking we have attained. Meditation can spare us the pitfalls of delusions about ourselves.

With meditation comes self-forgetfulness, thinking more in terms of one's relationship with God, and of serving God in others. The devotee must forget his little self if he is to remember that he is made in the immortal, ever-conscious divine image of God. The Bible says, "Be still, and know that I am God." This is yoga. "Be still" means to withdraw one's consciousness from the little ego and the body, from all desires and habits that pull the mind down into the lower spinal centers where the feeling of body-identification is strong. Only when one raises his consciousness to the higher centers of perception can he realize that he is made in God's image.

Don't be reluctant to sit long in meditation. The more you meditate, the more you will want to meditate. The less you meditate, the less you will want to meditate.

If you make the effort to establish the habit of deep meditation, you will find that your whole life will change. You will begin to bring into your life the spiritual balance that is essential. You will feel that God is guiding you, that He is behind you, sustaining you. He truly is. The only problem is that we don't *realize* it.

We have to throw off identification with the body in order to recognize that it is God who sustains us, whose energy pours through our bodies, whose intelligence works through our consciousness.

That is what meditation is—forgetting our mortal consciousness and remembering that we are immortal souls. In soul consciousness is the strength and the ability to accomplish anything in life that we want.

Don't be discouraged by anything. Problems come only to remind us that we need God in our hearts. Welcome each one. If life went smoothly for us we would feel no urge to seek God. We would forget Him. It is only when we are laid out flat by adversity that we yearn to be comforted. The ordinary man turns to his family and friends; but the devotee runs to the feet of the Divine Mother, and in Her finds his solace and freedom.

Attachment to God Decreases Material Attachments

Start your day right by first communing with God. End your day right by meditating deeply again, when the rest of the world has gone to sleep. Pray earnestly to Divine Mother to reveal Herself unto you; battle for Her attention if need be. Even if it is just for five or ten minutes, pray to Her with all the urgency of your heart, or mentally chant Her name. After meditation, go to sleep in the thought of Her. These practices help to uplift your consciousness. You will feel a divine calmness, a steady flow of peace and quiet within.

When you have made God the polestar of your life, and when you feel that your morning and evening engagements with God are the most important part of your daily program, you will become more and more attached to Him, and your attachment to the world will decrease. You won't lose interest in life, but you will be able to live free of its entanglements. Lord Krishna instructed us, "Be thou a yogi." That is, be so firmly established in the consciousness of God that your loyalty and devotion to Him are unaffected by the changing conditions of the world.

The devotee who would know God has to work at it earnestly and long, but with a childlike sense of faith in God. If you can stop in your daily activities for a moment and immediately feel divine peace bubbling within, if within your heart you can feel love for God and for everyone, then you may know that you are progressing on the spiritual path.

God Is Our Eternal Companion

The devotee should feel that the Lord is his personal companion—that whatever he does he is doing it with God. We should realize that we are not alone, that we never have been and never will be alone. From the very beginning of time, God has been with us, and throughout eternity He will be with us. Develop a more personal relationship with God by looking upon yourself as His child, or as His friend, or as His devotee. We should enjoy life with the consciousness that we are sharing our experiences with that Someone who is supremely kind, understanding, and loving. Only the Divine Being knows our thoughts even before we think them, and never turns aside from us, even when we are wrong, if we but seek Him out. That kind of love, that kind of understanding every human soul is seeking. But we have to do our part. Our beloved gurudeva, Paramahansa Yogananda, has said:

"God is found only through unceasing devotion. When He will have given you all material gifts, and still you refuse to be satisfied without Him; when you insistently want only the Giver, and not His gifts, then He will come to you....We are walking in the crowded lanes of life and occasionally we see some faces we know; but one by one they slip away. That is how life is. You and I are seeing each other now, but someday we will melt out of sight of each other. This is a tragic world, wherein all souls are tested, sometimes burned, in the fires of delusion. But those who conquer and say, 'I want only to know Thee, my Lord,' find God and freedom."

Take Your Troubles to God

*Self-Realization Fellowship international headquarters,
Los Angeles, California, March 31, 1961*

"Meditate! Meditate!" I say this to you all. Work comes second. Though you are very busy in your life here, following Gurudeva's example of great activity for God, meditation should come first. Remember that. I have never stressed anything different than this, nor did Guruji.

Think of the times in your life when you have idled hours away in useless talk, or in futile dwelling on negative thoughts. Henceforth, give such time to God instead. You may have psychological and emotional burdens—every human being does, until he becomes united with the Divine One—but so long as you whine about them and spread their negation, you will never make the ascent to God.

Whenever you are troubled about anything, do your best to correct what is wrong, but throw negative worry about it out of your mind. How? Mentally bow at the feet of God and place your problem before Him. Even before you bring your troubles to Him, He knows of them. Even before you surrender them to Him, He knows of your little crosses. The farther you have wandered away from the feet of the Divine, the heavier those crosses have become. If I could just impress this one idea upon you: Here you have to do with God and

Guru alone. Take your troubles to Them. Meditate more upon God. What ecstasy, what joy, what love you will feel!

Strive to manifest in your life more joy, cheerfulness, understanding, compassion, love. These come only from meditation that is deeper and deeper, and more regular. From the divine attunement you acquire in meditation, you will see how God and Guru guide you in everything you do. When your life is right with God and Guru, everything in your life will be right. You will always feel joy within. No amount of outward adversity will be able to rob you of that joy.

If you develop the habit of thinking that outer conditions are the cause of your unhappiness, or that other persons are responsible for your troubles, then I say you are missing the point of your life in an ashram. If each one of you cannot manifest cheer and joy and love in your life here, then you have only yourself to blame, only yourself. God helps him who helps himself. But He cannot enter a heart that is filled with doubt; He cannot manifest through a mind that is permeated with bitterness; there is no place for Him in the life of a devotee who is filled with negation. Remember that!

You have the time and the opportunity here to find God. This divine environment is perfect for such endeavor. But you alone make your heaven within; no condition or circumstance can deny you that sacred right.

Want God with All Your Heart

I have always strived to live by a principle that I learned many years ago at the feet of Guruji—the principle expressed in these words of Saint Francis: "Learn to accept blame, criticism, and accusation silently, without retaliation, even though untrue and unjustified." What a wealth of wisdom in that counsel! You do an injustice to your soul when you criticize others or when you concern yourself with others' blame or praise of you. What does it matter what people think? It is God's approval you want. Be filled with one wish, for God, God, God. Unless you are single-hearted, my dears, He is very hard to find. If you continually allow your mind to be dragged down into the mire of pettiness, of unkind criticism and egotistical judgment of your fellowman, you will never find God in this life. Why waste time? You haven't the time. As you get older you will realize it more and more.

If you want God, want Him with all your heart. He cannot and will not accept less than one hundred percent surrender on the part of His devotee. Christ proved that. Even his body, that most precious of man's treasures, he surrendered; and without anger or bitterness said: "Father, forgive them, for they know not what they do."

We should follow Christ's divine example of forgiveness and compassion. But in doing so we must not think, "Oh, I am so good, I am so noble; I magnanimously forgive my enemies." Spiritual pride is dangerous. There must be true compassion, genuine love in the heart. But we cannot have that without first loving God. Seek Him first. Love Him with all your heart, mind, and soul. And don't be satisfied until you have that divine love. Cry to God night and day; talk to Him unceasingly; be drunk all the time with the desire for Him, and you will see how wonderfully life changes for you.

The Spiritual Goals of Self-Realization Fellowship

Condensation of closing address, Self-Realization Fellowship Golden Anniversary Convocation, Biltmore Bowl, Biltmore Hotel, Los Angeles, California, July 12, 1970

Since I first set eyes on my guru, Paramahansa Yogananda, almost forty years ago, it has been my joy to lay my heart, my mind, my soul, my mortal form, at the feet of God, in the hope that somehow He might use this life I have given to Him. Such soul satisfaction has filled these years; it is as though I am constantly drinking from the fountain of Love Divine. I can take no credit for this; it is the Guru's blessing, a blessing he bestows on all of us in the same way, if we but prepare ourselves to receive it.

I ask you all to pray for me, and to give me your goodwill and blessings as I continue with you in serving this great cause of Self-Realization Fellowship/Yogoda Satsanga Society of India.

We are a part of the beginning of a great spiritual rebirth, or resurrection, that will encompass the world. I often read over the notes that I took when Gurudeva talked to us disciples. In 1934 he said that there will come a time when this great message from India will sweep the world, because it contains those immortal truths that are the very foundation of life and of all religions. To spread this spiritually liberating teaching is the purpose of Self-Realization Fellowship, the mission assigned to Paramahansa Yogananda by Mahavatar Babaji. Let us review briefly some of the "Self-Realization Fellowship Aims and Ideals."

To disseminate among the nations a knowledge of definite scientific techniques for attaining direct personal experience of God. The very first and foremost principle of Self-Realization Fellowship is to disseminate a definite science through the practice of which the followers of all religions may commune with God, and know by their own direct spiritual experience—not merely through the words of a scripture or great teacher—that God is.

Gurudeva used to say to us: "I can tell you what a jackfruit* tastes like, I can describe it, take it apart and examine it and tell you its various ingredients, as a scientist would do; but though I went on telling you about it for thousands of years, still you would not know the flavor of jackfruit. But if I give you a little part of that jackfruit to eat, you will say in an instant, 'Ah, yes! Now I know.'"

The same example applies to our relationship with God. The endless words, endless discourses, endless writings about God are not, in themselves, enough. Blessed are those who listen, and read, and heed those words. But above and beyond that, the message of Paramahansa Yogananda is that we must *taste* Truth. We must know God through direct personal experience.

To reveal the complete harmony and basic oneness of original Christianity as taught by Jesus Christ and original

* A fruit common in India.

Yoga as taught by Bhagavan Krishna; and to show that these principles of truth are the common scientific foundation of all true religions. In the name of religion, how many wars have been fought down through the ages! Truth is one, because God is one, though men may ascribe to Him various names. The mission of Paramahansa Yogananda is to show that there is one common highway to God, the route followers of all religions must take if they would reach Self-realization, God-realization. It is outlined in the next Aim.

To point out the one divine highway to which all paths of true religious beliefs eventually lead: the highway of daily, scientific devotional meditation on God. Thirty years ago Guruji said, "The day will come when the churches and the temples and the mosques will be empty." It is not the fault of religion, but rather the fault of its followers. So long as man will be content to go into an edifice merely to listen to a few words of truth and feel a little inspiration, and then go back to his home and continue the way of his ordinary God-forgetful nature—expressing, as before, the same moods, selfishness, nervousness, tensions, fears, and sensuality—of what value is his religion? The mission of Self-Realization is to encourage every man to establish within his heart a sacred temple for God alone, wherein he will in deep meditation commune daily with the Lord Himself.

To demonstrate the superiority of mind over body, of soul over mind. We seek to demonstrate that man is not bound by this tiny, fleshly cage. Jesus said, "Take no thought for your life, what ye shall eat, or what ye shall drink; nor yet for the body, what ye shall put on."* Do

* Matthew 6:25.

not pay too much attention to this physical form. Depend more upon the power of the mind and the power of God that is within the soul. We are not physical beings; indeed we are not even mental beings, though we operate through a mind and a physical body. We are the soul, an individualized expression of the Infinite Spirit. That is our real nature. The purpose of demonstrating this ideal is to tear ourselves free from all physical and hidden mental fetters that bind the soul to the flesh and to moods and leave us without peace.

To liberate man from his threefold suffering: physical disease, mental inharmonies, and spiritual ignorance. Only God-realization can free man permanently from all his suffering. Right action—in body, mind, and soul—balanced by right meditation is the formula for attaining that threefold freedom.

To advocate cultural and spiritual understanding between East and West, and the exchange of their finest distinctive features. Though this world is divided into East and West, God is showing mankind today that he can no longer live confined by the narrow boundaries of his own nation. Our Guru said, "God made the earth, and man made confining countries and their fancy-frozen boundaries."* God is showing us that selfish boundaries must no longer exist. But they cannot be destroyed by bombs and brute force. There is only one true way to dissolve those boundaries; you here are demonstrating that today. Boundaries disappear in united love for God as the Father of all. He must be the one common ideal, the one common goal, of all mankind. As we begin to

* Paramahansaji was quoting this and other lines from his poem, "My India," in his speech at the Biltmore Hotel on the night of March 7, 1952, just before he entered *mahasamadhi*.

recognize Him more as the one Source and Sustainer of life, fetters of prejudice fall away. We begin to see that those whom we thought were so different from us are just the same as we are. I have gone around this world four times now, and I have visited most of the major countries; in the people of each nation I see the same sweet sincerity, the same goals and needs, the same interests. Self-Realization must be the flagbearer of the message of divine brotherhood. When you go back to your homes, let this be your ideal. Let prejudices melt away. Receive all in that spirit of brotherhood, which is the true reflection of God in you.

To unite science and religion through realization of the unity of their underlying principles. There is no such thing as a difference between science and religion. Eventually both will arrive at the same conclusion: there is only one Cause. The material scientists are constantly striving to find the reason for this creation. Some deny the existence of God. But even an atheist, when facing some great trial in his life, will cry out involuntarily, "Oh, my God, my God!" Unconsciously he is clinging to the Eternal Principle that gives a sense of continuity to life. An Eternal Principle *is* guiding life; there are no "accidents." We are all here at this time because we were destined to be here now; and as surely as the sun and moon and stars travel through space at their own prescribed rate of speed and time, the life of each one of us is guided and protected by that great and lawful principle, God. "Are not two sparrows sold for a farthing? and one of them shall not fall on the ground without [the sight of] your Father."*

* Matthew 10:29.

To encourage "plain living and high thinking"; and to spread a spirit of brotherhood among all peoples by teaching the eternal basis of their unity: kinship with God. Seeking God and renouncing what Paramahansaji used to call "unnecessary necessities" does not mean embracing poverty. He used to say, "I don't like the word 'poverty'; it has a negative connotation. I believe instead in plain living. *Simplicity* is my ideal." Simplicity in heart, simplicity in speech, simplicity in possessions; purity that comes from an uncomplicated life and an uncomplicated mind; purity that comes from a direct and personal relationship with God, wherein you realize, "Lord, I have laid myself at Your feet. I am content with whatever You give me and whatever You do with me."

High thinking means to keep our minds always on that lofty level where at any given moment our consciousness can turn instantly to God. The mind should be kept always free from gossip, negation—anything that drags the consciousness into nervousness and restlessness. The mind that is filled with the thought of God is tranquil, and sees clearly into human nature and experience.

By leveling the conditions of life to the basic essentials for a happy and spiritually lofty existence, we find we have reached the one common denominator of life—God. We realize that we, and all beings, have come from God, that His power alone sustains us, and that to Him we will one day return. We see ourselves as a part of one great family of the Divine Parent; all humankind becomes our own, with no distinction as to race, color, creed, nationality, or social status. Imagine the world of beauty and peace that would blossom from a universal acceptance of this truth!

To overcome evil by good, sorrow by joy, cruelty by kindness, ignorance by wisdom. We cannot drive away darkness by beating it with a stick; it will vanish only when we bring in the light. Similarly the light of positive qualities and actions, and of Self-realization, alone can dispel the dark negative forces in this world.

What thrills me tonight is to see so much joy in you. When I first came to the ashram, I had the notion that seeking God was such a serious matter that there would be no time for laughter. But Guruji said to me, "Always be bright and cheerful, for that is your soul nature. You must be so happy in this world that you will never know sorrow, because sorrow is not a reality. Only God is real; and He is joy. Seeking God means the end of all sorrow." I have never forgotten those words. And so, when I see devotees with faces smiling brightly, and see the sweet and cheerful way in which they can laugh with one another, it fills my heart with joy, because I see we are following Guru's ideal.

To serve mankind as one's larger Self. The ideal of Self-Realizationists is to strive to live more in the thought of doing good to others, and less in the thought of "I, me, and mine." See how much joy you who have served this convocation have found in making this a happy and spiritually rewarding occasion for so many beloved members and friends from different parts of the world. You have helped to create this divine fellowship by the selfless way in which you have served them, forgetting your own weariness at times, and the little problems and stresses that are a part of carrying on such a large convocation. You have indeed expressed this ideal of serving mankind as one's larger Self. I pray that everyone here will embrace this selfless ideal, for it is in serving others that we learn to feel and to behold God in all.

This fiftieth anniversary is an occasion all of us will long remember. You will go back to your homes and you will often recall the sweet divine fellowship we have enjoyed. You are taking with you something of our hearts; and I believe that you are leaving here with us something of your own hearts—a mutual exchange. We have forged a bond of spiritual friendship, a divine relationship that will long endure; as we nourish it, it will become ever stronger, a great magnetic force that will draw many others to this sacred path of Self-Realization Fellowship.

In conclusion, let me read these words of our Guru: "My body shall pass, but my work shall go on, and my spirit shall live on. Even when I am taken away, I shall work with you all for the deliverance of the world through the message of God. Prepare yourselves for the glory of God. Charge yourselves with the flame of Spirit. If God were to say to me today: 'Come home!' without a backward glance I would leave all my obligations here—organization, buildings, plans, people—and hasten to obey Him. Running the world is His responsibility. *He* is the Doer, not you or I."

Divine Counsel

Words of spiritual guidance and inspiration. Unless otherwise noted, these selections are from talks at Self-Realization Fellowship international headquarters, Los Angeles, California.

God Is the Greatest Treasure

May 25, 1961

When you are lonely, cry to your Heavenly Father. When you yearn for understanding, run to Him. Man has little idea of what a tremendous Friend, what a tremendous Lover, what a tremendous Father-Mother-Beloved is seeking his love!

But you have to seek Him first. He will not impose Himself upon His children; He waits for them to seek Him. He will push in your path *everything* but Himself. He will offer constantly all kinds of substitutes, waiting to see if you will be content with them. If you are, you remain at a standstill on the spiritual path. But the wise devotee, like a naughty child, pushes aside every toy, every bauble of worldly attraction, and goes on crying for the Lord. Such a devotee finds God; none else finds Him.

I pray that you will all be naughty children of the Heavenly Father, crying inwardly for Him constantly. Don't let your minds wander into the mire of discontent

On the beach where grounds of Self-Realization Ashram in Encinitas, California, overlook Pacific Ocean

"Never have I asked for or craved spiritual experiences. I nly want to love God and to feel His love. My joy comes from eing in love with Him; I seek no other reward in life."

At Pahalgam, in the mountains of Kashmir, 1961

"That man truly lives who awakens with the dawn and filled with life, the joy of living, the desire to forget himself an express his greater Self, which is God within him. Until then h is merely existing."

and worthless distractions. Don't waste your lives like that, my dears! Be hungry for Him within, every moment. Be on fire for God. Convert all of your cravings into one massive flame of desire for the Lord. All your limitations will be consumed in that emancipating flame.

When distracted by worldly temptations, pray, "Lord, if I find material pleasures so enticing, how much more tempting must You be!" God is the greatest treasure. Every scripture declares it. Use your discrimination to shun lesser pursuits and to seek this one inestimable and eternal Treasure.

God Is the Answer to Every Problem

May 3, 1956

God is the answer to every problem that we face in life. We must cling more and more closely to Him. We must look to Him for guidance and for the solutions to life's riddles. Ultimately we must leave this body, so why give so much care to material concerns?

Give the greatest importance to seeking God and to serving Him. To serve God with a deep sense of self-surrender, and to have the consciousness of performing all our duties for Him, is a form of meditation, a way of seeking God. We must learn to find Him within our own consciousness, and to make Him our constant companion.

Gurudeva used to encourage us to gather in little groups to meditate, rather than get together to talk idly and waste time. You will find, as we did, that you have gained so much more by meditating with someone, or meditating alone, than by talking.

Avoid dwelling on the petty problems of life. Your most important concern is your relationship with God. Your emotions, your habits, what you think are your rights—these are not so important. Let God worry about them. You look after your attunement with God, and God will look after you. That is the divine covenant between the Mother and the child. Hold to that promise and never doubt that there is a divine law that takes care of everything.

Our only real relationship is with God and Guru. Hold to Their hand. St. Thérèse of Lisieux said, "I will spend my heaven in doing good on earth." This was also Master's promise. His one desire is to help us to find God. Whoever looks to him for guidance, whoever stretches out a hand to him for help, will feel without fail his guiding presence. You have to have faith, you have to do your part, you have to meditate; then you will arrive at perfect attunement to Guru's omnipresent help and blessings.

The Psychological Battlefield of Good and Evil

July 12, 1956

No matter how great the trials that come into your life, no matter what the tests, remember that Divine Mother is protecting you. We should not be surprised to encounter difficulties and struggles on the spiritual path. Sooner or later, they confront every devotee. We should face them bravely, confident in the knowledge that the grace of Divine Mother's love and protection is with us.

A battle between good and evil is going on within us all the time. Gurudeva used to say that the devotee stands in the middle, pulled from the one side by Satan, as the evil and negative forces, and from the other side by God, as the good and positive forces. Neither good nor evil can claim the kingdom of our consciousness save by the power to rule that we ourselves give. God has bestowed on us free will to accept or reject evil, to accept or reject good: to cooperate with God or to cooperate with Satan.

Divine Mother is standing behind each one of us, guiding and helping us, trying in every way possible through our conscience to help us make the right decision in the struggle on the psychological battlefield of good and evil. The wonderful blessing is that Divine Mother responds to every little effort, however small, that the devotee makes—every little effort to find God, to feel God, to be with God. We may not always be conscious of Divine Mother's response; but when we are in the midst of our inner battles, and we turn to Divine Mother for help, Her grace is there to direct our actions, to support our efforts, and to protect us with Her omniscient love.

Self-realization Is Found in Inner Silence

Ananda Moyi Ashram in Calcutta, January 18, 1959

Self-realization means the union of the soul with God. The experiences of enlightened souls in all ages have testified that the essential purpose, the ultimate goal, of all religions is Self-realization. Joy-permeated Ananda Moyi Ma, my gurudeva Paramahansa Yogananda, and all other great saints point to that one goal.

We should not become lost in the externals of religion—in rituals or forms. The purpose of *pujas,* masses, rites, should be simply to inspire devotees to seek God within. Otherwise such outer forms of worship are useless.

God is ever-existing, ever-conscious, all-powerful, ever-new Bliss—*Satchitananda.* The soul is ever-existing, ever-conscious, all-powerful, ever-new Bliss manifesting as individualized Being. By meditation one can realize this. Only by going deep into the peace within can we know the Self. Find some secluded place in your home or ashram and go within in meditation, and understand who you are. Then you shall know that you are made in the image of the Divine. From Joy we have come, for Joy we live, in Joy we are reborn. When we know this, then we have Self-realization. To attain this state, the feeling of blissful silence within is necessary. We can never know God through blind faith or outer forms of worship alone. We must take up deep meditation in order to reach God, and that is man's goal. Be with God now, and you will be with God hereafter.

We Have No Time to Waste

Self-Realization Fellowship Ashram Center, Hollywood, California, December 16, 1959, on Daya Mata's return from Paramahansa Yogananda's Ashrams in India

Our path is twofold: a path of service and meditation. Guruji said, "I believe in balance." He taught us to be calmly active and actively calm, to find God in the midst of all our activities as well as in the silence of meditation. The man who finds that balance is the man who knows happiness; he is the devotee who knows God, for God is both active and inactive—unimaginably busy as the Creator; ineffably still as absolute, blissful Spirit.

The ideal is to seek God in deep meditation and to find joy and happiness in serving Him. It doesn't matter in what way we serve. Whether we are working in the kitchen, or are teaching or writing—this is not important. What is important is whether we are doing it to please God or only for self.

My earnest prayer is that each of us may strive to feel within a deeper longing for the Divine Beloved. Go deep in meditation. This is the thing to remember. It doesn't matter if your meditation is only five minutes; make those five minutes count with the Beloved One. But meditate longer when you can. Seek no excuses for not meditating daily, regularly. Be on fire night and day with hunger for God. No words can describe the joy that comes through that relationship.

Seventeen months ago I went away from Master's ashrams in America to visit his ashrams in India. There was but one thought in my mind, "Thou art my life,

Thou art my love…"; my soul was afire with divine love. I have come back with that same feeling. We have no time to waste. Guruji used to say, "Life is like a dewdrop sliding down the lotus leaf of time." I often think how once that dewdrop begins to slide it moves ever more rapidly. For many of us, the greater part of our life is no longer in front of us, but behind us. I can feel only one thing: the urgency of using this time to know the Beloved within.

We should be ardent for God, on fire to find Him through our love and devotion, and on fire to serve Him. Don't be afraid to sacrifice the body, if necessary, in service to the Divine Beloved. God will sustain you. He is our strength. He is our life. He is our love.

And when you meditate, let your whole mind be absorbed in God. When you sit to think of Him, throw everything else out of your mind and plunge it deeper, deeper, into the omnipresence of the Infinite Beloved. From the Divine flows all the love that ever percolated through man's heart: the love of child for mother, of mother for child, of friend for friend, husband for wife. All forms of love have sprung from this one Source. Seek the Source. You have right here everything you need to find God. You do not have to seek further. Gurudeva brought the teaching to us. Now it is up to us to use it.

I am often reminded of these wonderful words of Master's, words we should live by:

> O Divine Beloved, I have nothing to offer Thee,
> For all things are Thine.
> I grieve not that I cannot give,
> For nothing is mine, nothing is mine.
> Here I lay at Thy feet

My life, my limbs, my thoughts, and speech;
For they are Thine, for they are Thine.

Gurudeva lived by these words. May we, his disciples, strive to emulate his example.

Be on Fire for God

January 18, 1960

Slothfulness and missing the point: avoid these two great drawbacks on the spiritual path. Over the years, we often forget the prime purpose for which we embraced the spiritual life. We become set in our devotional habits, following outward forms, but failing to keep alive the burning inner flame of desire for God. We gladly engage in many other pursuits, but become lazy about using our free time rightly: to deeply search for the Divine.

You are only rationalizing when you argue, "Well, if conditions had been different, if I had been treated with more understanding, if such and such a thing hadn't happened, I would today be closer to God." By such reasoning, you are missing the point. If you do not find God, the fault lies not with any outer condition or any other individual, but with yourself. In the ultimate sense, no person or condition can keep us from knowing God, if we strive always to free ourselves from sloth, indifference, and missing the point. Be on fire within for the Divine Beloved. And if you don't feel it, blame only yourself.

When I first came to Mt. Washington there were

many problems to face, with myself and with those around me. I was discouraged to discover that even in an ashram I couldn't escape these difficulties. But there was a tremendous fire ablaze within me to know God. I had great dreams of finding Him in this life. So I analyzed: "Can any condition, environment, or individual take from you your burning desire for God? If so, then you didn't really want Him very much." And with that thought in my mind I set about in great earnestness to direct my own steps aright on the path.

It is a tragedy when people get into such a rut that they lead the spiritual life outwardly, but allow indifference to extinguish their devotional fire for God. The devotee should start now to right such a condition by keeping the mind night and day on the Divine: God first, God last, God all the time.

Divine Love Makes Each Soul Unique

Arrival at Self-Realization Fellowship international headquarters from a visit to India, July 20, 1964

The tie that binds us all together so closely, even more than family ties, is divine love. The longer I live, the more I realize that this is the only force that can hold people together. To receive and communicate love, divine love, is our God-given duty in life. That love is already inborn, in our souls; and just as it is natural for the rose to give off a sweet fragrance, so it is natural for the soul to emanate the sweet fragrance of divine love. Again and again I remind the devotees, here and in India, of those immortal words of Guruji's that express the message of great saints down through the ages: "Only love can take my place." During my travels I talked with many people, and I found that love is the one message to which all human beings respond. The right level on which to approach all souls is divine love; and the way of divine love is the path our blessed guru, Paramahansa Yogananda, set before us.

Each one of us is unique in the eyes of God. And before Him we are all equal: there are none high; there are none low. We are all special to Him; because when He created each one of us, He thought not of anyone else, but of us alone. So we are individualized in His thought and in His great consciousness. That uniqueness of the soul is what we are to find within ourselves and to express. There is no greater way to manifest our uniqueness than through divine love, through our God-given ability to love purely and unconditionally. When we understand and practice this, it makes our path much easier. Once we experience the love divine that flows through us from God, it gives a glow to life that nothing else on earth—no powers, no glories, no amount of sense satisfaction—can give us.

Let God Help Carry Your Load

March 22, 1956

It is not the weak who find God, but he who says, "My Lord, I have given my life to You; I have surrendered my heart to You. Do with me as You will." I once said to Gurudeva, "What attitude can I take that will help me to carry the load I feel on my shoulders?"

"First of all," he replied, "do not think of it as a load. It is a blessed privilege to serve God." Even if it is just cleaning and scrubbing, discipline your mind to accept as a divine blessing the opportunity to serve wherever God puts you, whether it be high or low. Master added, "Remind yourself always that you are not the doer. God is the Doer; you are only His channel. Resolve to be a willing, receptive channel." When he told me these two things I thought, "Now he has given me this lesson, it is up to me to put it into practice." And I must say, it has enabled me to carry much more than I had thought possible. It will enable all of you to carry much more than you have thought possible.

Bring your consciousness into attunement with Divine Mother, so that She can carry that load—so that the weight of it is on Her shoulders. It doesn't belong to you. And when the time for meditation comes, everything else should go out of your mind, including all thought of the body. There should be absolute stillness within. It can be done, but you have to make the effort. Above all, you have to pray for the love of Divine Mother. Then spiritual effort becomes very simple. Use your weekends for meditation, for seclusion, to renew your spiritual strength within. If you meditate regularly and deeply, it will change your whole life.

Rely on God Alone

February 7, 1956

Our love for God should be wholehearted. Then it banishes the feeling of loneliness and dependence on human relationships. The companionship of the Divine One is incomparable.

It is right that we love others, but our reliance should be not on human beings, but on God. Anyone else we cling to, we lose. Maybe it is because the Lord wants us to know that if we would have Him, our attention on Him must be complete. It is wonderful to cry in the night for the one Divine Beloved of our souls; wonderful to utter to God all the things you long to say, knowing that He understands and silently responds.

I know now why Gurudeva didn't talk much with us about our personal problems. He wanted to speak to us only of God and to discuss with us only spiritual matters. He encouraged us not to dwell on personal problems, stressing that we could overcome those problems by seeking God. He would give interviews by the hour to visiting members, and I'd think: "Isn't that strange? The devotees around him seldom get a chance to speak with him about their problems." But he didn't want that relationship with us. He was training us to go direct to God. We may receive a little encouragement and help on this path by confiding in one another now and then; but when we need divine strength, we should go to God and God alone.

Guru is the divine channel through which the beloved Lord's wisdom and mercy flow. Like a mother bird that pushes the fledgling out of the nest so that it can learn to fly, the guru forces the devotee to establish his own relationship with God. For the same reason, God takes away from the devotee every human support, and everything material that does not awaken awareness of Him, until the devotee comes to the ultimate realization: "God is my strength, God is my love, God is my friend; God is my beloved, my only one. When He is absent from me, I am bereft of everything. I am a beggar. When He is with me I am filled with love and joy; I am filled with courage and strength."

If we go to human beings to find divine solace, divine comfort, we may for a while receive a little happiness and contentment, but sooner or later the Lord takes that prop away. We have to rely on God. He alone is everlasting, so He wants us to be strong in Him.

Give God a Chance

September 8, 1955

We should give God a chance to manifest in our lives; but He has no such opportunity when we hold on halfheartedly to the world and halfheartedly to Him. We must leave behind all else and take the supreme plunge into the Infinite. The saints tell us it is not difficult at all; that when we turn our thoughts and love within, we shall find the eternal, loving, joyous Companion who is always secretly with us.

I can remember coming often into Gurudeva's sitting room and seeing him there—his eyes shining like diamonds with divine love. All the disciples present could feel that he was absorbed in communion with

God. Sometimes in this state Master would speak aloud. We would hear him softly whispering to the Divine Mother.

Yet even though he was ever inwardly absorbed in God, I can think of no one who enjoyed everything he did more than Master. Nothing was ever drudgery to him. He was very creative; and whatever he did was performed with the greatest interest, because God was ever present in his consciousness, and his whole desire was to please Him.

Again and again Master repeated his spiritual counsel to us: meditate deeply every day and *feel* the presence of God. We are here not just to become well versed in this great Yoga philosophy of Self-Realization, but more importantly, to *live* it. Through Master's grace and instrumentality we have been given this blessed opportunity.

Admonitions for Advancement on the Path

March 7, 1956

During his last days with us, Gurudeva left for all the disciples several admonitions to follow for greater advancement on the path. He touched upon a number of subjects.

He counseled us to be more serious and yet more cheerful: "Be happy and cheerful within, but don't engage too much in joking and lightness. Why waste your inner perception in useless talk? Your consciousness is like a milk pail. When you fill it with the peace of meditation you ought to keep it that way. Joking is often false fun that drives holes in the sides of your bucket and allows the milk of your inner peace and happiness to run out."

Master taught us not to sleep too much, but to use that extra sleep-time for deep meditation and God-communion. "Sleep is only an unconscious way of enjoying the peace of God's presence. Meditation is the state of conscious rest and peace, more refreshing than a thousand million sleeps."

"Don't waste your time," he said. "No one else can give you the deep desire for God that keeps you steadfast. You must cultivate it for yourself. Don't intellectualize and don't rationalize; above all, never doubt that God will come to you. When duties are done, give your time to God in meditation, and you will experience inwardly His divine bliss, His divine love."

Divine Love Is the Motivation of Right Activity

June 11, 1968

I strongly believe in the ideal of right activity along with meditation. In right activity the heart, mind, and soul are joyously united. There is no feeling of, "I'm doing You a favor, Lord," but of joyous dedication to God. In right activity one does not look for any fruits of his actions, but acts just for the joy of doing for God. That joy of doing comes when you are in love. You can't go through life without being in love—with something! Every human being thrives on love. The way to enjoy the greatest love throughout your lifetime is to seek the one Cosmic Lover, the Eternal Beloved of our souls. That has been my experience; it *is* my experience. To me, God is the only reality in this world.

Wise is he who keeps his mind engrossed in the Cosmic Beloved. You don't know what a lover that Divine One is until you learn to walk with Him, to talk with Him, and to understand that He is your own. Then you know what joy is; then you know what love is in its highest and most beautiful form. That God is love is the very core of the message of our gurudeva, Paramahansa Yogananda.

True, Self-Realization is a path of wisdom, it is a path of work, it is a path of bliss; but above all, to me, it is a path of divine love. Divine love so transforms the human being that he can no longer think in terms of "me" and "mine," but only of "Thou, Thou, my Lord."

Each one of us should take this message of love to our souls, and strive to live it.

The Delusion of Mortal Consciousness

All-Day Christmas Meditation, December 23, 1960

To attain the greatest results from meditation, it is important to dismiss from your mind during meditation all consciousness of the body, and all restless thoughts. This we can do if we fully understand that we are not this body, we are not this mind. Through countless past lives we have worn many bodies and many minds. Try to take the consciousness beyond identification with this particular little body cloak we wear now, this particular garment of mind that we are using temporarily. We are the immortal soul, made in the image of the Most Beloved.

Let your heart hunger for God, as it has never hungered before. We have spent incarnations wandering down the pathways of desires—for name, fame, glory—for all the things of mundane worth this life has to offer. During meditation today, cast out from your mind every thought but one: "My God, I am made in Your image of wisdom, of bliss, of love. I am Your child. Free me from the delusion that has made me think of myself as a mortal being, and let me behold myself—as Gurudeva and all of the great ones have beheld themselves—as Thy child, Thy beloved child."

The Privilege of Serving God

October 9, 1964

No one in this world is indispensable. God can very well do without the services of any of us. I recall again and again these words Guruji said to me many years ago: "Don't ever give Divine Mother the feeling that you are doing Her a favor by the work you do." His words struck me very deeply then, and they mean even more to me now; I realize that serving the Divine Mother—as we do in carrying on Gurudeva's work—is a rare privilege. But any time we think we are doing much, we have the wrong attitude. We should be filled every moment with humble gratitude for the blessing of being able to serve Her.

Service must be given with right attitude. Without right attitude no amount of labor means a thing to Divine Mother. We may feed the poor, or give counsel, or perform endless other useful tasks, but if we begin to think: "How many good works I am involved in! Isn't it marvelous that I can do so much to help others? And how people appreciate it!" then the attitude is wrong. Master often reminded us: "Divine Mother is watching the heart." She hopes we will want to please Her, rather than concern ourselves as to whether or not we are pleasing man. Man's opinion will change: today he gives us his love and regard and tomorrow he may cast us aside. Man's devotion is not noted for its constancy. We should therefore dwell upon what is truly important: pleasing the Divine, who is our eternal Friend.

Goals for a New Year

January 1967

As we begin the activities of the new year, may we realize the importance of utilizing every minute to improve and perfect ourselves as divine children of God. Now is the psychological time to analyze our actions during the past year and see what spiritual progress we have made. We should think deeply about what we want to change in ourselves and in our situation in life, and then do our best to carry out our aims. We should write down the good resolutions that will help us to achieve our highest aspirations in the coming year, and then review them every month with the idea of assessing whether or not we are achieving the goals we have set for ourselves.

In this new year may we understand more fully

that finding God is the only permanent solution to whatever problems we face in life. We should cultivate deeper awareness of Him.

The only real relationship man can have is with God, and with the guru as His channel. It is God who disciplines us; it is God who loves us. Be faithful to Him! And cling to the Self-Realization teaching as to the hand of our blessed Guru. His one great desire is to help us become reunited with our Heavenly Father.

We Are Bound Together by Love

Eighteenth Anniversary Commemoration, Self-Realization Fellowship Ashram Center, Hollywood, California, April 21, 1969

It is in the consciousness of love divine that Gurudeva Paramahansa Yogananda has drawn all of us together. With the strong but gentle thread of love he has bound us together to form a fragrant garland of devotion, of love, to be offered at the feet of the One Love, the Supreme Beloved of our souls. He has inflamed our hearts with a burning desire for God, because he has kept always before us the ideal that love for God must come first, then, in the spirit of that love, love for all others. That divine love is what he referred to when he said to me, "…I want to see you all so drunk with the love of God, night and day, that you won't know anything but God; and give that love to all who come."

The Divine Mother as Disciplinarian

March 1, 1956

Divine Mother has a many-sided nature. How She appears to us is only a reflection of our own state of consciousness. When we are in tune with Her, She is the blissful, loving Mother. When we are out of tune, She seems to be a strict disciplinarian. It isn't that the Divine Mother wishes to discipline us. Suffering comes from separation from God. It is we who create that separation by our forgetfulness of God, by following our bad habits, by becoming too much involved in outer things or in our emotions and moods. Divine Mother never forsakes us; it is we who forsake Her. Then She seems like a stern disciplinarian, but only because we have severed our connection with the Source of all that is right and good.

So when Divine Mother seems to have vanished from our attention, to have escaped from the orbit of our consciousness, the trouble lies with us, not with Her. Perhaps our mind has become too absorbed in worries, which is a spiritual sin, for it shows lack of faith, lack of trust in God; or too wrapped up in sensitive feelings, which comes about when we are identified with the ego and think of ourselves as mortal beings, rather than as the divine image or soul; or too much involved in worldly pursuits. It is at these times that Divine Mother leaves us. She says: "Where I am, My child, there thou shouldst come." Divine Mother hides Herself not to punish us, but to encourage us to strive to lift up our consciousness to the divine realm where She exists. She wishes us to keep striving to improve ourselves.

Master's training was like that, too. Just when you thought you had stretched yourself, so to speak, or had lifted your consciousness to a certain level, Master raised the standard a little higher. "Now that you have come this far, try to reach even higher." To meet the new standards, we were constantly trying to improve ourselves; trying to throw off the consciousness of the body, the consciousness of limitation, the emotions that bind us to this mortal frame. The purpose of the guru, the divine teacher, is to help lift us out of ourselves. He helps us to cast off the lower self, the ego, and remember that we are created in the immortal image of God—ever-existing, ever-conscious, ever-new Bliss and Love. That is what we are, and we ought to feel ashamed if we are not able to manifest our true nature every moment of our existence. Perfection is what we must strive for. Then Divine Mother will no longer need to pose in the aspect of disciplinarian, but will continuously manifest to us Her pure form as the joyous, kind, understanding, loving Mother.

Bringing Out the Best Within Us

Janakananda Ashram Chapel, SRF international headquarters, February 28, 1962

If you have not yet felt intense yearning for God, do not be discouraged; make it a point to meditate more deeply every day, even if it's only for five minutes. Call on God, as Guruji used to say, as a drowning man gasps for air, as a dying man struggles for breath. If you have that sense of urgency, you will know God in this lifetime. To cultivate this feeling of immediate need for God you must meditate daily and nurture other good habits.

You cannot remove darkness from a room by beating it with a stick. Switch on the electric light and the darkness disappears. In the same way, repression of wrong habits is not the most effective way to overcome them. Rather, turn on the light of understanding that comes from deep meditation, and from a voluntary conscious effort to practice self-control. In the light of self-discipline and wisdom the darkness of wrong habits vanishes.

Everything in this world is thought; so if you wish to dislodge a certain bad habit, begin mentally affirming to yourself, in a positive way, the opposite good habit. If you have a tendency to be too critical, the moment you catch yourself unnecessarily finding fault with someone, think about his good points instead. Very often, the impulse to criticize stems from jealousy, a sense of insecurity, or egotism. It is not necessary to concern yourself with others' failings; only your own. Fault-finding destroys your peace.

Always look for the good in everyone. This doesn't mean we should be Pollyannas, closing our eyes to the wrong others do; that attitude shows only a lack of discrimination. But there is such a thing as becoming so critical that we cannot even see the good in others.

Man is full of imperfections. Why concentrate on them? Master took each devotee as he was, and concentrated upon bringing out the best in that disciple. And do you know how he did that? By giving the devotee love and understanding. And that is what we should do. We should strive to help one another to change for the better by exercising the divine soul qualities of love and understanding that are within ourselves, bestowing them freely on all.

The Power of Discrimination

March 21, 1962

The only way we can escape this terrible wheel of *karma,* on which we are going round and round like squirrels running on a treadmill, is by adhering to the spiritual path and ideals set forth by our blessed Gurudeva, and knowing that his blessings and guidance are never absent from us. In his omnipresence in God, he is just behind the darkness of our closed eyes, silently beholding us. As we retain this consciousness, which keeps us receptive to his ever-present help, we shall increase our ability to use the sword of discrimination he has given us in the wisdom of his teachings. We shall bravely cut away the worldly distractions that coax our minds onto materialistic pathways. We shall be able willingly to choose to live by those ideals that draw us Godward. By the power of discrimination we learn to do the things we ought to do when we ought to do them—not impelled by any external influence, but acting calmly and wisely with our God-given intelligence and will.

We should learn to examine ourselves every day: "How am I faring? Which way am I going? What have I done this day that has taken me Godward in thought, speech, and deed?" And "What wrong habits am I continuing to follow that take my mind away from God?"

When again and again, by meditation and by constant spiritual effort, we remind ourselves that we are not mortal beings but immortal souls, we gradually break apart the chains that have long bound us to the limited consciousness of flesh and to a world of ceaseless disruptive change. Once we begin to slough off those fetters, we have glimpses of ourselves as souls made in the image of God. The more we behold this divine image within, the more we feel His love in our hearts, His wisdom in our minds, and His joy in our souls.

Watch Your Own Thoughts and Actions

January 28, 1962

Guruji used to say to us, after we had meditated: "Remain quiet, be withdrawn. Even when you leave your meditation seat, let your mind rest constantly, or as often as possible, in the thought of God." In that thought we draw the strength, the wisdom, the great love that our souls hunger for. Be mentally anchored in that which alone is changeless in this changing world: God.

When one gets to know his real nature, he becomes a bubbling ocean of joy within. And he is so desirous of holding on to that joy that he is careful to avoid displaying it too much outwardly, lest it be lost.

Be always kind and loving. Get away from petty thoughts, from smallness. If others are unkind to you, try to win them by your love. If that doesn't work, then give the problem to God and forget it. This is the way to get along in the world.

Each one of us should strive to manifest divine love. We are not to concern ourselves with whether or not others are manifesting this love; if we base our behavior on that of others we will never overcome the small self. We have to seek to maintain a higher consciousness for ourselves. If that lofty ideal is always in your mind, and if you are concentrated on your own striving, you will have no time to think whether or not others are following this ideal, or doing their part. Your concern should be only for your own actions, and your own state of consciousness, whether you are inwardly racing to the feet of the Divine Beloved.

A Pattern for Spiritual Living

January 1961

How can you know when you are progressing spiritually? Within you there is always a deep longing for God. When you meditate you are able to bring the mind under control so that the attention is focused on the object of your meditation. You feel a great ocean of peace within you and all around you in the universe. While living your daily life there is a constant desire to try to do good, to try to do what is right. In the mind there is always the thought, "Lord, bless me, guide me, help me to know Thy will. Help me to find Thy love."

In one sense it is a very simple thing to find God—it is a way of life. Get up in the morning with one thought: God. Carry out the whole day's activities striving to the best of your ability to avoid anger, selfishness, resentment, criticism, knowing full vell that in all your experiences it is the Divine with whom you have to do. He is your support; He is your defense; He is your strength; He is your love. Seek to please Him first, last, and always, and in pleasing Him to please Guru and your fellow beings. The last thing at night, meditate deeply.

So many times when our bodies would be weary, Guruji would look at us and say, "Never mind; it is good for you to work hard for God. But you should not use that as an excuse not to meditate at night. Do with less sleep. And if you have only fifteen minutes to meditate, make those fifteen minutes count. Again and again throw the world out of your consciousness and plunge into the great ocean of God's presence within."

To find God is easy when we have but one purpose, one goal—God alone. To find God is very difficult when we permit our minds to wander and become lost in unimportant things. Know what you want and then go after it wholeheartedly. If you want God, be on fire to reach Him. If your body stands in the way or resists you, discipline it. In meditation, command the body to sit up straight and be still; watch the breath,* and don't let your mind go to sleep. The mind must be like a live wire when you meditate; your whole attention should be afire. And if you ask how to get to that state, I tell you that there is a very easy way: cultivate a personal relationship with God by talking to Him every moment. Our minds are always focused on something—pleasure or pain, ideas that catch our attention, or personalities.

* Reference to a specific yogic technique of meditation practiced by Self-Realization Fellowship students.

Focus your mind on God instead. Be in love with Him night and day. If you can't feel that love, pray for it unceasingly. What a wonderful state it is to be in love with God! like a silent, gentle, joyous river flowing continuously through your consciousness, uniting your being with the great ocean of God's presence within and without, all around.

The Secret of a Happy Life

December 18, 1962

The world within* is the only real escape from our tribulations. The more one remains in the divine consciousness of the inner world in meditation, the more one wants to remain in it. It is easy to understand why great yogis immerse themselves in that meditative state for hours, days, or years at a time. When one goes deep within, he realizes that only then is he truly living, only then is he in touch with Reality. There is no wish to leave that inner heaven, to come down from that plane of consciousness. The only reason for doing so is to carry on one's God-given duties in the world.

The Lord does not expect us to fly away to forests to seek Him in solitude. We must find that solitude within ourselves. Then, when we bring our consciousness back from the meditative state to awareness of the world, we remain on a higher plane and can better fulfill the will of God. Being unattached to the fruits of our actions, but performing all our duties with the deepest

* "Neither shall they say, Lo here! or, lo there! for, behold, the kingdom of God is within you" (Luke 17:21).

earnestness, the most conscientious attention, the greatest zeal; seeking results not for ourselves but only to fulfill the will of God—this is the way to find peace in the world.

Gurudeva once said to me: "The secret of a happy life is just this: Always say to yourself inwardly, 'Lord, Lord, not my will, but Thy will be done. Thou art the Doer, not I.' " When you strive to live by this thought, you arrive in time at a nonattached state of great inner freedom. You harbor only one wish: "Lord, I want to do only Thy will. Whatever that may be, it is satisfactory to me, because there is nothing in this world I want to achieve for myself. I strive only to perform whatever work Thou hast given me to do, solely to please Thee."

The Divine Romance with God

April 7, 1955

Be so strong within, so completely absorbed in the thought of God, in complete faith in Him, that nothing else matters. Then no hurt, no upsetting incident, can shake you. They are merely tests. If the body is afflicted, it is to goad us into remembering Divine Mother and our true nature in Her. From physical tests we ultimately learn to pray, "Though this body is racked with pain, though I am uncertain of what lies ahead, O Mother, I know that I am not this body, but the immortal soul that for just a short time dwells within this mortal form." And if the mind is tortured with doubts, and the soul feels unfulfilled, it is only a reminder that we must turn to the Infinite Source for the security and fulfillment that our heart craves, for the love that no human relationship can give us. Naught but God alone can fully satisfy the innate cravings of the human spirit.

It is God from whom we have sprung; it is God and God alone for whom we should live and work selflessly, ever more selflessly; and it is into the arms of our beloved God that we shall one day melt again. Think of this truth and hold it always before you.

Don't be afraid of anything. Don't be afraid of the body's struggles. Don't be afraid to make some sacrifices, and to surrender yourself to God. This is a great lesson each devotee must learn. Why be so solicitous of this temporary body? Surrender it to God.

I can remember the days when I used to hold back, thinking too much of self. What tremendous freedom you feel, once you cross that barrier and realize that it is Divine Mother who sustains us every moment of our lives, through every breath we take in, through every throb of our hearts. If She is with us, who or what can be against us?

In each one of us is the Divine Spark that was in all the saints. God loves us not one bit less than He loves them. Then wherein is the lack? Only within us. If we cannot feel God's love, it is because our love for Him is not deep enough. Where does the fault lie? Again, only within ourselves. We have no one else to blame—not our circumstances, or our environment, or the people around us. We must meditate more deeply.

When you get up in the morning, meditate. If necessary, mentally whip the body to make it obey you. After all, the body is with you for only a few years, to be used as an instrument of your immortal soul, your true self. Discipline the mind also. Once you bring body and mind under control, you will find it so simple, so easy, to realize the presence of the Divine.

No matter what you are doing, there is nothing to keep you from silently conversing with God. While there is yet time—while there is life, health, opportunity, and freedom to have this divine romance with God—don't be satisfied until you feel God's love well up within you every time you think of the Divine Name. "Will that day come to me, Ma, when saying, 'Mother,' my eyes will flow tears?" When Guruji used to sing that song, my heart would yearn, "Oh, Mother, will that day come for me?" Only that love is real. Our highest duty in life is to find that love and to awaken it in the hearts of others. For this reason alone does this organization of Self-Realization Fellowship exist. As a devotee of this path, hold that ideal always before you.

Recordings of Talks by Sri Daya Mata

Many of Sri Daya Mata's talks are available on audiocassette. Descriptions of each title can be found in Self-Realization Fellowship's catalog of books and recordings (see facing page).

Audiocassettes

Anchoring Your Life in God

Finding God in Daily Life

Free Yourself From Tension

God First

A Heart Aflame

Is Meditation on God Compatible With Modern Life?

Karma Yoga: Balancing Activity and Meditation

Let Every Day Be Christmas

Let Us Be Thankful

Living a God-Centered Life

Moral Courage: *Effecting Positive Change Through Our Moral and Spiritual Choices*

Strengthening the Power of the Mind

Understanding the Soul's Need for God

The Way to Peace, Humility, and Love for God

Videocassette

Security in a World of Change

Books by Paramahansa Yogananda

Available at bookstores or directly from the publisher:

SELF-REALIZATION FELLOWSHIP
3880 San Rafael Avenue • Los Angeles, CA 90065-3298
TEL (213) 225-2471 • FAX (213) 225-5088

Autobiography of a Yogi
Man's Eternal Quest
The Divine Romance
Wine of the Mystic: *The Rubaiyat of Omar Khayyam—A Spiritual Interpretation*
The Science of Religion
Whispers from Eternity
Songs of the Soul
Sayings of Paramahansa Yogananda
Scientific Healing Affirmations
Where There Is Light: *Insight and Inspiration for Meeting Life's Challenges*
How You Can Talk With God
Metaphysical Meditations
The Law of Success
Cosmic Chants

Audio recordings of informal talks by Paramahansa Yogananda

Beholding the One in All
Awake in the Cosmic Dream
The Great Light of God

Other books from the same publisher

The Holy Science *by Swami Sri Yukteswar*
Finding the Joy Within You: Personal Counsel for God-Centered Living *by Sri Daya Mata*
God Alone: The Life and Letters of a Saint *by Sri Gyanamata*

A complete catalog of books and audio/video recordings is available on request.

Free Introductory Booklet

The scientific techniques of meditation taught by Paramahansa Yogananda, including Kriya Yoga, are presented in the *Self-Realization Fellowship Lessons.* For further information, please ask for the free introductory booklet *Undreamed-of Possibilities.*

AIMS AND IDEALS
of
Self-Realization Fellowship

As set forth by Paramahansa Yogananda, Founder
Sri Daya Mata, President

To disseminate among the nations a knowledge of definite scientific techniques for attaining direct personal experience of God.

To teach that the purpose of life is the evolution, through self-effort, of man's limited mortal consciousness into God Consciousness; and to this end to establish Self-Realization Fellowship temples for God-communion throughout the world, and to encourage the establishment of individual temples of God in the homes and in the hearts of men.

To reveal the complete harmony and basic oneness of original Christianity as taught by Jesus Christ and original Yoga as taught by Bhagavan Krishna; and to show that these principles of truth are the common scientific foundation of all true religions.

To point out the one divine highway to which all paths of true religious beliefs eventually lead: the highway of daily, scientific, devotional meditation on God.

To liberate man from his threefold suffering: physical disease, mental inharmonies, and spiritual ignorance.

To encourage "plain living and high thinking"; and to spread a spirit of brotherhood among all peoples by teaching the eternal basis of their unity: kinship with God.

To demonstrate the superiority of mind over body, of soul over mind.

To overcome evil by good, sorrow by joy, cruelty by kindness, ignorance by wisdom.

To unite science and religion through realization of the unity of their underlying principles.

To advocate cultural and spiritual understanding between East and West, and the exchange of their finest distinctive features.

To serve mankind as one's larger Self.